BLACK LIGHTNING PRESS
PRESENTS FOR REVIEW

914 Hover Ridge Circle
Longmont, Colorado 80501
303.776-8400 - Telephone
303.776-8633 - Fax
Email: Book@TheDreamRider.com

Title: DREAM RIDER: Roadmap to an Adventurous Life
Author: Rosemary Carstens
ISBN: 0-9740546-9-0
Pages: 128
Price: $15.00
Publication Date: June 2003

A copy of your review to the address above will be appreciated.

DREAM RIDER

Black Lightning Press

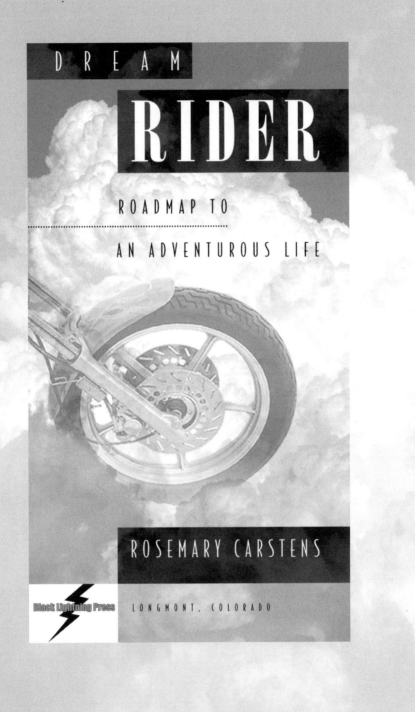

DREAM

RIDER

ROADMAP TO

AN ADVENTUROUS LIFE

ROSEMARY CARSTENS

Black Lightning Press LONGMONT, COLORADO

BLACK LIGHTNING PRESS
914 Hover Ridge Circle
Longmont, Colorado 80501
303.776.8400 – Telephone
303.776.8633 – Fax
Press@TheDreamRider.com
www.TheDreamRider.com

© Copyright 2003 by Rosemary Carstens
First Edition
Printed in the United States

Cover Design: LLPrindle Design
Digital Photography: Peter Warren

Women's Studies/Travel Literature/Motorcycling
ISBN 0-9740546-9-0

For Katie and Steve
Always.

Contents

Hold fast to dreams, for if dreams die, life is a broken winged
bird that cannot fly.
— Langston Hughes

Introduction

Have you ever looked back over your life and thought how subtly or boldly events have played a role in steering your course? By the age of four, I was reading. Every payday my father brought home chocolate-covered cherries for my mother and comics for me. I had a stack in my closet almost as tall as I was. Delighting in the characters of Archie, Donald Duck, Uncle Scrooge, Superman, and others, I was quite fussy about my "books" and didn't want anyone messing with them. Soon, with my mother's help, I moved on to discover the captivating world of real books.

I still have a dozen books dating back to my years from five through twelve—among them, *The Little Lame Prince,* written by Dinah Mulock in the late 1800s. My edition contains charming black and white and color illustrations and on the inside front cover is a painstakingly drawn cursive, "Miss Rosemary Guymon, Age 9." I was completely captivated by this story of a lonely, handicapped prince who flew off on a magic cloak on dozens of adventures of discovery:

> The minute the window was opened, out it sailed— right into the clear, fresh air, with nothing between it and the cloudless blue. Prince Dolor had never felt any such delicious sensation before…to him even the level plain looked beautiful. And then there was the glorious arch of the sky, with a little young moon sitting in the west like a baby queen…the evening breeze was so sweet and fresh….by and by a few stars came out—first two or three, and then quantities quantities!

I read and reread that book, marveling each time at the wonder of sailing through the air to anywhere in the world you wanted to go. A very imaginative child, I daydreamed constantly of magical things like flying, becoming invisible, and walking upside down on the ceiling of my house. I daydreamed over and over about flying. Years later on my first night flight as a pilot, I would feel the same delicious sensation as Prince Dolor had on his first flight.

The second defining moment in my life happened in the second grade. My teacher, Mrs. Locke, a robust woman thoroughly immersed in life, opened my eyes to a world beyond my provincial farming community when she shared with our class some handmade, tin Aztec masks purchased during a summer spent in Mexico. Sitting at my small desk in my frilly dress, Shirley Temple curls springing outrageously around my head, my lust for adventure, my curiosity about other people's cultures and far away destinations burst into flames that would later lead me to explore many remote regions of the world.

By the time I was ten years old, I had resolved that I would learn to fly when I grew up—and go everywhere on earth! I believe my lifetime passions for adventure, traveling and cutting through rushing air by car, plane or motorcycle were born in these two epiphanous events.

From childhood onward, certain attractions and passions have been caste in my path like crumbs leading the way through the forest—and I have snatched them up eagerly and stuffed them in my mouth. Has it been fate then, carrying me away on so many adventures and into sports like scuba diving, flying, and motorcycling? Certainly my early experiences, active curiosity and imagination played a large role in fantasizing about these things, but in reality I was a product of a generation of women who generally did not venture beyond the confines of a traditional American definition of womanhood.

Many women who grew up in the post-WWII years and the idealized decade of the fifties (when traditional roles for women were still held sacrosanct) married right out of high school or went to college to meet their future husbands rather than to establish a lifelong career. Being "la-dylike" still ruled behavior and choices. Although closer examination in later years would prove that many of those absolutes were seriously flawed, or extremely rare in real life, the permissible ways of fulfilling the role of womanhood would continue to influence us in varying degrees for the rest of our lives. We were pressed into a ready-made mold—and it would be very difficult to escape.

As the sixties, the Vietnam War, civil rights, and women's liberation, rolled in waves across the far horizon and into our lives, we were fired with new possibilities that excited and invited. But somehow, for many of us, even as we swam on the crest of these new ideas, embraced them and experimented, we found it difficult to throw off the framework in which we had been raised. We are the bridge generation. We have lived with one foot mired in traditional expectations and the other testing the waters of alternative lifestyles. We are the translators between generations. As the decades passed, a vast majority of us continued to put our personal fantasies on hold and allowed our private dreams of adventure to wait in the wings at the edges of our lives.

For thirty years, I have gone up against the "nice girls" legend. It took twenty years amidst career, marriage, divorce, and children, to move from being a high school drop-out to graduate school. I learned to fly and to scuba dive, then did both solo in the United States and abroad, at a time when few women were accepted into the sports. I have frequently traveled to remote regions of the globe, often solo, to seek adventure, to see what is on the other side of the mountain. But every single time, I was torn between the magic of my fantasies and my fears of injury, death, loneliness and failure. Every time. I am not a natural athlete, nor particularly physically fit. Where others seem to jump into new sports with grace and agility, taking on new adventures without a backward glance, only my persistence and determination have carried me through—one baby step at a time.

At the age of fifty-six, my imagination was captured by a dream of becoming a motorcyclist. Why I did it and how, how I dealt with the disapproval of family and friends, stuck with my dream of touring the country on a motorcycle, and what I learned about myself and others in the process is one half of this story. I realized I wanted to share what I had learned about following one's dreams regardless of social expectations and gender or age biases. This is not a book for those to whom goals come easily, for super athletes. It is a book for other women like myself who are afraid of change but drawn to it, who wish to define themselves rather than have others do it. Women who are willing to take the steps to move from longing to living in spite of their fears. Over the many months it has taken to complete this project, I have met hundreds of women of all ages and from all types of backgrounds who have shared the dreams in their hearts with me—dreams of adventure, achievement, change and alternate journeys. One such group of more than sixty women have served as my informal advisory council in writing these chapters. Every one of them began riding motorcycles after the age of fifty, many when they were in their sixties. In total, we have ridden hundreds of thousands of miles. We have shared our stories, our disasters and our challenges, and they have enriched my understanding of life, made me laugh and cry, and encouraged me every step of the way in completing this book. They are the Dream Riders.

I hope this book will be a source of inspiration and encouragement to women of my generation, as well as to those heading up the hill to the big five-oh, and to those who traveled through this decade before me. To ride their own dream. To become the person they fantasize about being. In sharing my tale, I hope other women will be motivated to extend their own horizons, to examine the boundaries of their lives and to consider emigration into new territory.

In each chapter I have tried to provide insights into the process of reaching for an unorthodox dream, the changes life brings to each of us, the dynamics of aging, and doing the best one can with what one has to bring to the party. In the final chapter, titled "Seasons," I will share with you my perspective on the transformation that comes with achieving a cherished goal and the empowering nature of living a fully engaged life. I hope each of you will feel inspired to share your perspective with me as well. There is a synergy in sharing experiences of growth and transformation with one another that expands exponentially—it becomes enriching to all of us to an infinite degree.

The fallible and wistful Pinocchio sings about wishing upon a star for your heart's desire, as dreamers do. This is a book by a dreamer, for other dreamers, about the fun and excitement of making your wishes come true.

1

The possible's slow fuse is lit by the imagination.
— Emily Dickinson

You don't get to choose how you're going to die, or when.
You can only decide how you're going to live now.
— Joan Baez

Falling in Love
with the Dream

What are your daydreams? Queen of an alternative universe? Las Vegas showgirl? Whipping all comers at the U.S. Open tennis championship? Arriving at the office one morning, charging straight into your boss's office and single-handedly tweaking his obstinant, pointy little head until it faces in a whole new direction? At heart, most daydreams are about escape, achievement, or more control over our own lives. They can also be just plain fun!

My mind runs freely, like a dog on the loose looking for chow in all the wrong places. I never let reality get in the way of "Let's Pretend."[1] In the best of my fantasies, I am always an action goddess—strong, beautiful, athletic, loved and admired by all. Of course, many of these stories I act out in my head as I go about routine daily chores are not anything I would really try to do. I just take pleasure in imagining them. But, now and then, an idea begins to replay itself insistently, to demand I do something to bring it to life. Such was The Case of Motorcycle Fever.

In my fifty-sixth year, I got braces on my teeth, went back to graduate school, and met The Deuce. A civil engineer with a weakness for buxom blondes and fast motorcycles, he was called "Deuce" because deuces are wild and often pretenders. As it turned out, he was an express bus making a quick tour through my neck of the woods. During this excursion, I saw some beautiful Colorado wilderness from the back of his motorcycle, and it would prove to be the beginning of a passionate love affair—not with the man, but with a motorcycle named Sinbad.

Riding with The Deuce I had begun to notice every motorcycle on the road and any news about them. In August of each year, hundreds of thousands of motorcycles roll across the United States headed for the annual Harley-Davidson Rally and "run-what-you-brung" Races held for a week in Sturgis, South Dakota. Motorcycle aficionados around the world know "Sturgis" as a siren's call. Anyone who loves the sound of thundering pipes feels the urge to make this pilgrimage at least once, if only to say they've been. I had come across the rally website while surfing the net and found myself totally distracted by pictures crowded with big, hairy men and scantily clad women astride powerful, shiny motorcycles. The bikes were gorgeous, compelling, and dangerous looking. The bikers riding them were like pirates—edgy, ear ringed rebels with the open road as their cause. I instantly calculated that if I left home at six the following morning I could be in Sturgis by mid-afternoon.

Most people ride motorcycles to Sturgis—it is a point of honor to "ride your own." Only a wanna-be drives a car. But I didn't let the lack of a bike hold me back—by this time my daydreams were breaking through into "gotta do it." Throwing my Harley boots and some black jeans into a bag, I headed north. The closer I got, the more motorcycles I saw converging on this one small town.

There is a visceral excitement and energy generated by the sights and sounds of more than 350,000 big, bad bikes funneling in from all directions for wild times in the Black Hills, including thousands who annually visit from overseas. They come to honor the iron ponies, to race, fight, drink, gamble, trade, swap lies and generally party hearty. It is the sound of thunder, the rumble and roar of mechanical horsepower, a raw sexual energy with the routines of daily life stripped away and dreams of being a renegade come to life. It feels like a chance to write your own legend.

How was the Sturgis Rally? Well, I have to admit that I have always considered myself a liberal—but, in that scene,

I was definitely a conservative. I saw more tattooed flesh on display than at a Sumo wrestlers' convention, and most of it should have remained covered in the name of environmental decency. Bare breasts, bare butts, bare bellies—and every imaginable (and unimaginable) item of black leather clothing. Outrageous was the name of the game and everyone was a player. The five short blocks of Main Street in this small Midwestern town (from the corner of Junction Avenue west to Fifth Street) completely jams with motorcycles of every color and model, both stock and fantastically customized. Here, Harley-Davidson is king of the road, the American definition of two-wheeled cruising. I saw Softail Customs, Super Glides, Knuckles and Pans, easy rider choppers, Boss Hogs, and more. Every other brand name is considered a runner-up at this event, but they were there— from Motoguzzis, Indians, and Goldwings to Viragos, Big Dogs and Victorys. Themes of skulls, American flags, wolves, women with impossible physical attributes and even more improbable postures, plus a wide variety of other concepts, find illustration on tanks, bodies, posters and clothing.

A thousand motorcycles lined each side of the street facing outward, each a scarce two feet apart. The chrome was blinding. In the middle of the street there was a double row of hundreds more, with an "aisle" on either side allowing a moving pathway through the crowd. From dawn until late into the night, these aisles buzzed and rumbled with people parading their bikes and themselves in a constantly changing tribute to the great American motorcycle. It was, "See and be seen, baby—it's *happening!*"

For forty-nine weeks out of the year, the buildings along these five blocks are the usual small town fare: hardware stores, insurance offices, drugstores, cafes, and ordinary retail shops. But for the week of the annual Rally, and a week before and after, that all changes radically. Storeowners rent out their places for $5,000 and up, depending upon location—and city permits to display items runs $125 ($500 if you want to sell anything). Motorcycle parts, photographs, tattooing, food and drink, and every conceivable item that can be imprinted with a motorcycle, a party motto, or the official emblem of the year is offered for sale. There is big time money in this for the locals and a year's income for those who bring their goods to market. Since its inception in 1938 as a local weekend of low-key racing and rallying put on by the Jackpine Gypsies riding club, until the event caught fire after a CBS piece on it in 1971, crowds have continued to build. At the 60th anniversary event held in 2000, attendance was estimated at between 550,000-633,000 and, that same year, the City of Sturgis collected a total of $286,000 in sales taxes. Every possible accommodation and campground is sold out within a 200-mile radius. Many of the mere 6,400 residents in this town leave for the rally period and make thousands of dollars a week renting out their homes for blocks around Main Street.

I walked the streets for hours, checking out bikes, bikers and biker babes, leather goods, food booths, and all the weird and wonderful vendor products reflecting the biking culture. I even broke down and wore a couple of my own new purchases, trying to look as though my big old Harley was parked just around the corner! I considered how a tattooed rose might look, but couldn't figure out what body part to put it on that would be guaranteed not to sag. Social niceties of everyday life fall by the wayside here. Where a man or woman might check out a person of the opposite sex discreetly on the street at home, here the gaze is direct, appreciative, and speculative. If you are going to be offended by candid sexual interest, this is not the place for you.

Amazed by the number of women driving the biggest and most powerful of machines—Low Riders, Fat Boys, Wide Glides and Road Kings, to name a few—I realized it had never occurred to me that a woman could manage one of these 650-plus pound bikes. A light began to shimmer in the back of my mind. Although memories had faded of rides as a passenger on several motorcycles in my distant youth in southern California, now I recalled that wonderful thrill of freedom riding through the curves on a mountain road. I had never thought to do it again, until fate brought The Deuce into my life for a brief spin on the wild side. Being in Sturgis, my mind and heart reverberated with new possibilities for adventure.

Sturgis was a surreal trip, a foreign film in loud, uninhibited color. The variety of people and activities ranged from the raunchy to the amusing, from the obscene to the bizarre. The scene was simultaneously entertaining, shocking and exciting; you checked your judgments at the town gates and just let it flow! It was avant-garde Biker Theater in full regalia, and I wanted a walk-on part. I went, I saw, I fell in love. One year later, I would return—riding my own.

My fantasy had poked its head through the thin membrane between dreamtime and real time and was demanding attention. The dream had been identified and it was time to figure out whether this was something I could really do. I felt fear and I felt excitement—the tension between "do it" and "forget it" had been cranked up a notch. I was ready to take the Thunder Road.

---

1 "Let's Pretend" was a popular Saturday morning kids show of the forties, the inspiration of Nila Mack, who developed a company of versatile juvenile talent to play a variety of changing roles in fairy tales week after week. She was known as "the fairy godmother" of radio.

2

You must do the thing you cannot do.
— Eleanor Roosevelt

Consider the postage stamp, my son. It secures success through its ability to stick to one thing till it gets there.
— Josh Billings

Learning to Ride and Other Challenges

Returning from Sturgis with the thunder of revving engines still roaring in my ears, my dreams and thoughts were filled with the excitement of all I had seen. I was totally engrossed in the details of this parallel universe, as fascinated as if I had fallen completely in love with a new man. I wanted to know everything about the machines, the riders, the culture of motorcycling and, most of all, the women who did this on their own. I realized I was irresistibly drawn to the idea of joining them.

In my daydreams as I drove home from the rally, as I returned to my regular, steady, everyday life, I rode a big black machine with lots of shiny chrome and rumbling exhaust. I was dressed all in black leather, my blonde hair flowing freely behind me; I was on the open road headed for adventure with a capital A. Driving along in my boxy 1993 sports utility vehicle, I was a female Walter Mitty, hauling ass in glorious freedom on the highway ahead of me. Little did I appreciate at the time the vast difference between the dream and the reality.

We all have our daydreams of adventure, success, and escape. Who has not dreamed of what they would do if they won the lottery? The dreams themselves are a pleasure and, often, our minds take us as far as we really want to venture into our fantasies. All my life, probably stimulated by my love of adventure books and movies, I have starred in my very own mind movies, a woman of courage and beauty who saves hostages, survives enemy attacks, leaps buildings with a single bound—you get the idea. What is it that occasionally takes us from the dream toward the reality? This time, for me, it was the growing question hovering at the edge of my fantasies: Could I possibly do this?

I am not a naturally athletic woman. In the late fifties, when I was a teenager, girls were not encouraged to pursue athletic achievements. Sports were a part of the physical education programs, but expectations were low—as was our consciousness about female athleticism—and there was a much greater emphasis on being ladylike than on doing your personal, physical best. As a saying of the times went, "Horses sweat, men perspire, and ladies glow!" We were groomed to be spectators, to play adoring, supportive roles for the men who would enter our lives and for the families we would nurture. To some extent, we were like windup dolls—programmed to perform certain functions, but requiring a male before any initiation of activities could occur. Real life did not begin unless a man pushed the start button.

I don't feel any bitterness about the realities of those times, although there is regret for the possibilities I didn't know existed. It was simply the way it was, the cultural framework within which both young men and women grew up. Rock and roll was just catching fire, the questions and the demands of the sixties were still ahead of us. In the fifties, mainstream American culture appeared to be a gentle wave, calmly cresting before running gaily out across the sand. In reality, the wave would rise higher and higher, to become a surfer's dream and a swimmer's nightmare—complicated, dangerous, ripping the surface in every direction, crashing in a huge, violent onslaught of the shore, altering it forever.

What does all this have to do with a woman learning to ride a motorcycle? It is all about perceived possibilities. Women growing up as I did often have the dream of adventure, but still feel some fear or taboo about fulfilling that dream. Even today, women often measure their dreams with a yardstick of societal approval or disapproval, against what is considered acceptable.

In talking to many women and men who ride motorcycles, I am struck by the statement from most of the men that they simply decided they wanted a bike, bought one, got on, and rode—often with physical mishaps along the way. One male biker friend, who is an instructor for motorcycle safety courses, told me that men feel they have a "motorcycle gene," that it is unmanly to take a riding course, that they are supposed to know how to do anything having to do with mechanics or vehicles. In my conversations with women bikers, they generally seem to feel more comfortable with the reinforcement and encouragement of being taught the skills that will make them competent and safe riders. There exists a mythology that women would not come naturally to any sport involving a motorized vehicle.

Well, I fit the myth—I felt uncertain I could physically handle a motorcycle or learn the skills needed to make my fantasy a reality. I have always learned physical skills slowly, but I also knew my strengths in learning them were my determination and persistence.

Several national organizations are devoted to the development of skills and the promotion of safer motorcycling in the United States. An initial eight hours of classroom instruction covers the basics of the mechanics and operation of motorcycles and is followed by eight hours or more of field time in which students operate school-owned bikes with engines averaging about 250 ccs. There are specific, approved exercises that must be successfully completed before you can pass the course. In Colorado, passing the course allows you to proceed to the Department of Motor Vehicles, take a simple written exam, skip the operational portion, and receive an official motorcycle operator endorsement on your driver's license. I decided to take the course and, if I passed, purchase a bike and take up the sport. Naively, I expected to be an expert biker babe when I received my endorsement.

My class met on two Thursday nights for classroom work and on two Sunday afternoons for riding. The first night of class, I was both nervous and excited. There were about thirty people in my class, of all ages and all levels of previous experience. Many had ridden motorcycles and dirt bikes for years but had never gotten a formal license. Some were motivated by the need for cheap transportation, the desire to try something new and exciting, or the wish to participate more actively with a rider spouse or boyfriend. Many of my classmates already had bikes.

At least two-thirds of the students were women, most in relationships with male riders. I was the oldest student in the class by at least ten to fifteen years. That part didn't bother me in the beginning, as I have always been enthusiastic about learning new things whether or not I fit the stereotype of those usually participating. I learned to pilot airplanes and to scuba dive in times when it was unusual for a woman to be involved on her own in either activity. There was only one other woman in flight school with me; no other women in my diving classes. I am never a shining star in any sport, but manage to obtain a sense of accomplishment, enjoyment and joy from the endeavor. Because learning new physical skills is a challenge for me and does not come easily, I particularly value each hard-won step along the way. Learning to handle a motorcycle would prove no exception.

Let's face it—most people of either gender do not take up motorcycling at the age of fifty-six. The fear of breaking bones and incapacitation in general has set in; we are well aware that we are, indeed, mortal, and that good health is truly a blessing not to be taken for granted. By this age, most of us have at least one or two little glitches in the hardware and they are beginning to manifest themselves. For me, the vision of myself dressed in sexy black leather, wind whipping through my blonde hair as I downshifted through a curve on a beautiful mountain road was enticing and dazzling. The reality would prove to be a long time in coming.

I thought my biggest stumbling block would be my vivid imagination; every example of what could happen if you were not sufficiently alert or skilled on the street played itself out in my mind in full color—mostly blood red. I was unprepared for how tough it would be for me to master the physical requirements of riding. My legs were literally shaking the first Sunday on the riding range. The little 250cc bike seemed enormous, powerful, and capable of inflicting disastrous physical damage.

The class was large and was divided into two groups: those who had ridden and those who had not, or had little experience. The instructors paired those in my group off. We were to take turns pushing our partner in a straight line while he or she "steered," just to give us a feeling for what that would be like. From my view, bent over, huffing and puffing as I pushed with all my might, I had been paired with the biggest rear end in the history of biking! I was worn out after the first exercise.

The second exercise involved starting the engine in neutral, then shifting into first gear, slowly releasing and engaging the clutch as we inched across the blacktop with both feet on the ground. When I had first chosen my "ride" for the day, a beautiful shiny black Honda Nighthawk 250, the instructor told me it was brand new and he didn't want anything broken on it. So, I was being extra careful. As I crept in fits and starts across the blacktop, the more experienced group of students gathered to watch our uneven progress. The extra attention was more than my nerves could bear—I turned the handlebars in some unexpected way, the bike began to fall, I couldn't hold it, and down we both went in a heap of steel, chrome and humiliation. Lying on the ground, I opened my eyes to see a round, black plastic object just inches away—I had broken the new bike—God save me from the wrath of Instructor Jerry! I was unhurt but lay there a moment contemplating that broken part. Jerry raced over, hauled me up, and yelled at me for what would be the first of many times, "Why did you look down? *Never* look down—you go where you look!" My legs were trembling, and I was on the verge of tears when I responded in a shaky voice that I had broken the new bike, pointing to the offending part. Jerry reached down, picked up the bit of plastic, threw it off to the sidelines with disgust, and said "So what? Get back on and ride."

From that moment on, I knew that Instructors Jerry and Bill might be a little rough around the edges when it came to social graces, but their yelling and frustration had one source—they were determined to teach us to be the safest bikers possible, to save our sorry behinds from unnecessary accidents, to build our confidence and skill level so we could enjoy the thrill of the sport without ending up a statistic on the highway. Hour after hour we rode the course in summer temperatures hovering around 100 degrees. We rode circles, ovals, around the rectangular course perimeter, figure eights—first in one direction, then reversing and riding them all in the other. We did easy takeoffs and stops, wove through cones, did directed swerves, learned to pick up our speed, shifted gears, and practiced emergency braking. At the end of a section on the riding course, my mind felt numb, I was sweaty, exhausted, had long lost my edge and any energy reserves. I prayed I would not be the worst student in the class—and I did not drop my bike again.

One student never learned to control her bike and struck fear into all our hearts when she headed in our direction. One man could not follow directions, did not listen, and consistently performed poorly in the exercises. Thank God for them—they were the answer to my prayers not to receive the lowest score in the class. One woman performed flawlessly—she rode as though born to the sport, with skill easily acquired and grace of movement. She received a perfect score. She was my hero.

After a couple of hours on the range, I felt my age in spades but was determined to push on through. I arranged for a couple of extra hours of private instruction and it helped a lot. My imagination and my fears were my biggest stumbling block. Rather than relying on what I knew mechanically to be the means to effective performance, pictures of terrible accidents would flash through my head just before I tried a new exercise. And, after a few hours, my physical exhaustion affected my performance as well. But I progressed. I was thrilled when I rode freely around the course, when I kicked it up to second gear for the first time, when Bill or Jerry yelled "Yes!" when swerving was easy for me. I fought the machine rather than working with it, trying to steer and manhandle all that poundage around instead of simply pressing in the direction I wanted to go, easing the clutch off or the brakes on. When I finally completed the class, I was unable to write or do small functions with my right hand for two weeks. I had gripped the throttle so hard in my attempt to make things work that I had exhausted my hand muscles. Riding a motorcycle is not about how strong you are—it is about skill, grace, and mental alertness, combined with common sense and proper maintenance of your machine. Being too tense, or too afraid, works against you.

One of the things I have realized over and over again as I have pursued this sport, as I have tried to force things to happen, is how it mirrors so many of the lessons of life. Trying to micromanage anything in life seldom reaps rewards. It is impossible to control everything around us, whether mechanical or relational. Concentrated effort to try to control all aspects of our world can prevent us from fully functioning in our lives. We can only approach each task with as much wisdom, skill, and good humor, as possible; then, fate plays a role, as do the interactive choices of all those around us. It's a wild ride, we do the best we can—and it's worth it.

Finally, bikers' graduation day arrived. As I wheeled off the course for the last time, after a five-hour stint of graded exercises, the group gathered to receive their certificates. All but two passed the course. I managed a mid-range score and felt proud to have done so. The star performer of our class received her perfect score. Bill and Jerry cautioned us all that this should only be the beginning of our training, that we needed to continue honing our skills, take refresher courses, and consider the experienced rider course after one year of riding. They said that not all of us were ready to go right out on the road. The next day I was at the Department of Motor Vehicles when it opened at 8 a.m., breezed through my written exam, and received a very satisfying red letter "M" on my driver's license. Visions of riding danced through my head, and soon, very soon, I would meet the bike of my dreams.

3

When people keep telling you that you can't do a thing,
You kind of like to try it.
— Margaret Chase Smith

When choosing between two evils,
I always like to try the one I've never tried before.
— Mae West

Finding My Ride

I had passed my class—time to buy a bike. I read the classifieds, talked to friends who had motorcycles, and haunted the dealerships. Growing up in the fifties in southern California, an 'old fashioned' girl, my ideal motorcycle was a chopper style straight out of "Easy Rider,"—chromed, flamed, raked, and black, of course. This meant a Harley-Davidson and I spent a lot of time at bike shops casually throwing my leg over one monster machine after another to see which one "sat" the most comfortably. I wore my black leathers, strolled around checking out the paint jobs and prices, straddling a bike here and there and wrestling it majestically to an upright position, as I envisioned myself roaring down the road. It was great visual projection, thrilling to consider, fun to pour over the specifications of each bike and discuss them interminably with other biker buddies—but the reality was, I was nowhere near ready to handle one of those major hogs.

During The Deuce's whirlwind tour of my neck of the woods, I had ridden as a passenger on the back of his Yamaha Virago 1100. It had style, reliability, and was big enough to look like a real motorcycle and not a scooter. It was low enough that I could easily sit astride it and have my feet touch the ground with a slightly bent knee on each side. I decided I should consider the Virago for a first bike.

An ad appeared in the Albuquerque Journal for a 1994 Yamaha Virago 750 being sold by a private party who was just moving up to a Harley touring bike. In the biking world, there are several categories of street machines: primarily sport, cruiser, and touring bikes. Each category has its loyal and fierce supporters and there seems to be chemistry involved in their preferences, just as in liking blondes, long legs, or cute butts. You feel drawn to a certain style or image and that's it. For me, it's cruisers. The Viragos are cruisers. The difference between the 750cc and the 1100cc is slight, other than engine size. The body style is just the same; the weight of the 750 at more or less 430 pounds dry is only a few pounds lighter than the 1100, and it has a little less fuel capacity. The difference in horsepower generated by the two is about fifty-five for the 1100 and forty for the 750. I must admit that I wanted to buy a bike that would not be disparaged by owners of bigger bikes for its lack of power—and yet I really didn't think I was ready for anything too powerful. I decided to check out the 750.

There is a gender thing about motorcycles, as there is about ships. Many men, and some women, refer to their bikes by the feminine pronoun, as in "she really leaned sweetly through the curves. . . ." For quite a few women riders, their bike is a "he." I can only speculate as to the sexual implications of the genderizing of mechanical objects. But, for me, my motorcycle was always fully male—strong, reliable, sexy, and exciting.

The previous owner had the Virago parked out at the curb when I arrived—its paint was a deep, metallic green that shimmered in the sunlight, its other parts were totally chromed out, there was a gleaming triple light bar up front, and a set of deep-throated Cobra after-market pipes detailing the lower lines of its frame. "He" was absolutely gorgeous, and it was love at first sight!

I had my checkbook in my hand as I climbed out of the car and was a goner before I had even sat on him for the first time. Sinbad would be his name, and he and I would set off over the next year on many an adventure.

Although no one could have made me believe it at the time, Sinbad and I would travel over 11,000 miles during my first year as a biker babe. Motorcycling would become my main recreational activity, and Sinbad my main traveling companion, through good weather and bad, in the mountains, the desert, and across the flatlands and rolling farmlands of Colorado, New Mexico, Wyoming and South Dakota. We would ride to the call of the road and encounter a variety of interesting fellow travelers along the way. We would be buds, Sinbad and I, on calm, sunny, dry cruises, through sand storms and wind-battering, tense and frightening rides, and across slick, wet, highways. I would become a weather vane—watching daily weather reports; watching the sky for signs of approaching storms; checking flags, roadside grasses and trees for signs of wind strength and direction.

I would find there is a "Zen" of motorcycling.[1] On the road there is plenty of time for contemplation, for mulling over one's life or just life's journey in general. You journey with nature; you are completely exposed to it physically and you develop a keener sense of yourself as a fragment of the whole, not as captain of the universe. You meet many people from such varied walks of life. You learn to try harder to suspend judgments based upon appearances.

In spite of the rough appearance of many bikers, there are thousands of responsible, decent people out there who simply love the sport as I do, who are called to "the thunder." We want to escape the stereotyping of our everyday worlds, to experience the sense of adventure lying ahead, waiting for us, down an unknown road. We are weekend warriors, if you will. It is our response to the dehumanization of a world run by dollars and numbers. We can feel free on the road to live out, if only in our imaginations, our individual destinations and fantasies. We are man, woman, nature, and machine—mostly uncomplicated by the more frustrating aspects of so-called modern and urban life.

In these thorny days of conflict and uncertainty, when demands upon our time seem never ending, women can feel boxed into conformity. That doesn't mean we don't want to attend to our professional and family responsibilities, that we don't love and honor our regular lives. But a part of us longs to feel our heart sing, our spirits lift—and for some of us women that happens on the open road with the wind in our hair and horsepower at our command. It's a thrill. And I am glad to have had Sinbad as my companion on the trail.

1 This refers to a classic "read" for motorcycle enthusiasts, *The Zen and Art of Motorcycle Maintenance*, Robert Persig (Bantam Doubleday Dell Publishing Group, 1975).

4

Life's a Journey, not a destination.
— Aerosmith

No one but Night, with tears on her dark face,
Watches beside me in this windy place.
— Edna St. Vincent Millay

Rosita & the Four Supremes

The Canyon Cruisers Easter Run to the Carlsbad Caverns in southeastern New Mexico was my first big ride; we would cover 750 miles in three days. Since buying Sinbad, I had been practicing persistently. It had been slow going. The extended forks and increased horsepower of my Virago, compared to the Nighthawk I had ridden in class, was intimidating and I had managed to pronk it into a crash barrier my first time out. With a cracked rib and lots of scrapes and bruises, I looked like I'd wrestled an alligator and lost, but I held the dream. I kept practicing and took a private class with David Smith, an outstanding instructor in Albuquerque, where I was attending graduate school to become either a Latin American specialist or a Biker Babe *par excellence.* The latter was winning, the road called constantly, and slowly my skills improved but my confidence remained shaky.

A word here about "handles." These are the nicknames that bikers adopt (or are given) to express aspects of their road personalities. I had come to be teasingly known as "Rosita Bandita" among my riding friends, mostly as a reference to my studies and interest in all things Latin American. Toward the middle of March, one of those friends, "Frenchie L'Orange," came up with the wild proposal that a ride from Colorado down through New Mexico at Easter time would be a great trip. "Buffalo Bill" Holbert and "Big John" Phelps signed on. They invited me to join them and I was thrilled! Next, a guy by the name of "Cool Hand" from southern Colorado, with more than 400,000 miles of riding under his belt, joined the crowd dedicated to riding and romping in the great southwest. As departure approached, the excitement built, and by midweek—as bikers say—all were "good to go."

So there I was in Albuquerque with a mere 1,500 miles and one crash to my credit, pretty good in town, shaky in the wind and at speed, but loving to wear black leathers and looking forward to riding with the big dogs. I got my nails done, polished my boots and my bike, fluffed up my hair, and headed out. I spent the first night in a motel only forty miles out of town, jumping up every hour to check on my bike. Buffalo, Frenchie and Cool Hand were camped out under a full moon in Villa Nueva after a long, hairy haul from Colorado against killer winds. Frenchie called to say they were all howling at the moon, having a blast, expecting hangovers in the morning, and would be a little late getting to Kline's Korner. No problem.

Day One of my big adventure. I packed up and rode to Kline's early. I walked in, hoping I looked ravishing and slightly dangerous in my black leathers, bandanna, knife and boots. There was open-mouthed awe—or was that disbelief? The Tres Hombres, as they referred to themselves, came waltzing in forty-five minutes later and we ate and chose our route for the day.

Outside gusting winds were blowing trash and dust around, an omen of what was to come. We saddled up and headed south on Hwy 54 toward the town of Corona. The narrow two-lane road wound through desert, scrub, and miles of open country. The wind kicked up a notch and I began to wonder what I was doing out there struggling with Sinbad and trying to keep pace with such experienced riders. I remembered my instructor warning me to stay home if the winds were over 25 mph—these were waaay over! I was out of my league but the Tres Hombres just motored on, macho to the end. Suddenly, coming up to a curve and over a rise, with traffic approaching, a powerful gust moved my bike across the road into the oncoming lane! For a moment, I panicked. I thought about how much I liked gardening, movies, and other quiet pursuits. I prayed. I contemplated letting go. In the few seconds available, I made my decision, my training kicked in and I countersteered into the wind with all my strength, swerving back into my lane, over-correcting, going on—rapidly signaling with my turn signals that I wanted to get over, off, out of this! The guys ignored me because there was nowhere to pull over, the shoulders were soft sand, and we had to go on. After a mile or so, we arrived in Corona and pulled into the lone café. I got off my bike and began to shake all over, cry, and retch. The three biker guys hauled me into the café by my curls and sat me down in front of a hot chocolate, all the while rolling their eyes around and congratulating themselves on a cool ride! I watched the woman sweeping the floor and plotted taking her job and living on in Corona, never to ride again. They weren't hiring.

Decision time. Two of the Tres Hombres zoomed off into the wind headed south. I sweated and fretted, told Buffalo Bill I didn't think I could go on. He suggested I pull into the gas station about a hundred yards down the road and make my choice—stay in Corona until the wind dies down or go on with them. I started off at a wobble, cast a long appraising look at the crumbling motel at the side of the road, the one café, the half-dozen other weather-beaten buildings, gritted my teeth, squinted my eyes, hunched my shoulders over the handle bars, revved the throttle—and rolled onto the highway. Frenchie and Cool Hand had turned around to see what was taking us so long and passed us going the other way; Bill signaled for me to pull over and wait up for them. I stop for no man. Once I go, I go.

Praying all the way, countersteering for all I was worth, ticking the miles to Carrizozo off one by one, I careened over dusty hills, and through drab green scrub; I skirted rolling tumbleweeds as big as my bike, and crabbed into the wind. Frenchie and Vern finally caught up and took the lead again—they glanced at me as they passed and, being seasoned veterans of the gender wars, gave me a wide berth. Finally, finally, under huge, gray, threatening thunder clouds, Carrizozo and its one coffee shop—Four Winds Café, what else?—appeared at a crossroads. Never has a greasy burger, a sticky tabletop, and coffee boiled thick and black on a Bunn server ever looked so good!

The rest of the first day was easier. We headed east toward Roswell, fighting brutal winds all the way. Just when we got the hang of that and felt a little more relaxed, we hit the rain grooves. Miles and miles of rain grooves. Even the grooves had grooves. Every once in awhile, there would be an unridged stretch of highway and we would breathe a collective sigh of relief—just before we hit the next section of rain grooves! We wound through the little town of Lincoln in Billy-the-Kid territory and the "boys" let me take the lead. It felt good leading what I thought of as "my" banditos through this historic town of the old west. The highway here winds up and down through low hills; there are piñon pine and deciduous trees, a checkerboard of farms and ranches, a glint of water off to the south—pretty country when you could take your eyes off the rain grooves.

Roswell was a welcome sight as we pulled into the Budget Motel—we probably weren't. Three unshaven, smelly gringos and one fuzzy headed, pale, sweaty "gringette" on four motorcycles rumbling thunder. They put us back by the alley out of sight. One difference between the sexes I discovered on this trip was that biker scum goes "as is" to the bar immediately upon rolling in and unloading their gear. I want it on the record that this woman showered and put on clean clothes. Still, when I finally joined them in the bar for my shot of tequila Gold and a beer chaser, they were a heartwarming sight. These were my comrades; they had seen me through one of the most physically challenging days of my life. Only once had they rolled their eyes (where I could see them anyway) and asked each other what a woman was doing there. They never again mentioned me lying on the ground shaking and whining about the wind. They had seen me through.

As we sat there swapping lies, rehashing each groove and mile of wind and vibration, slurping down beer and gobbling spicy piles of nachos, the fourth hombre was fighting his way down to Roswell. Big John, a man who prided himself on his ability to shift his mighty beer belly from side to side for ballast as he rode, would hit town the next morning ready to rock and roll.

Day Two. A beautiful sunny morning with only a light breeze in the air. Breakfast at 7:30. The Tres Hombres decided to do a quick reconnaissance ride to see Bottomless Lakes Campground while I waited for John to show. First, all bikes were lined up for group photos, recording our trip for posterity—or evidence, depending on how things went. Now the wind was getting meaner. By the time Big J roared in with his Cobras steaming and thundering, we knew God wanted to test us but we set off south for Carlsbad anyway. Nothing stands between a biker and his road. As Cool Hand says, "There's always a headwind!" Let's hit it guys. I began to feel I was getting the hang of it—had I ever ridden perpendicular to the highway? Naw, I was cool, I was a biker babe, I was…sick of the wind! Did it ever stop blowing in this blasted corner of New Mexico?

When we arrived in Whites City where the caverns are located, the wind was roaring mightily and pushed us around the parking lot until we settled in a heap together by the front entrance. We lunched down in the main cavern area, 750 feet below the surface. I am claustrophobic and kept trying not to think about how much rock was pressing down over my head. I tried to think about being in a wondrous place, about how I would soon see stalactites and stalagmites of pornographic proportion—that is, I mean, phenomenal proportion. Sights beyond imagination. Wrong! The four gringos went gleefully through—I reversed direction and went up 750 feet to wait where I could see the sky and cease my cold sweat. I've climbed mountains and dived oceans, been chased by diving Skuas in the Antarctic, and had fire ants charge up my skirt in Africa—I'll take all that any day—just don't make me go into a dark, oppressive cave! Sitting there waiting for the guys to surface, I realized that it was getting darker outside and not from nightfall—a full-fledged sand storm was scouring the outside of the building with a vengeance. Oh Boy! I could hardly wait to ride 125 miles in that!

We headed out with Big J warning me I had better go heavy on the throttle or I could get stuck out there in the sand after dark. I had never ridden at night and I didn't want to start then—I wanted my shower, my clean clothes, my tequila and beer chaser—I wanted my mother! We agreed that John, Frenchie, and Cool Hand could ride hard ahead if they wanted to, and that Buffalo Billy would keep pace with me. Poor Bill—probably lost the draw back in the cave, stuck with the newbie. By this time I was taking John's advice and rolling on throttle at every moment I felt I could. Sand penetrated the side openings of my face shield and gritted across my eyeballs. The wind swirled and bobbled my helmet, doing its best to rip it and my head off of my shoulders. I leaned over low, trying to get a modicum of protection out of a windshield the size of a dinner plate. I counted off miles on my odometer. Boy Howdy was this fun.

Finally, just at dusk, we arrived back at the motel—me too whipped to even say thanks to the Buffalo Kid, just shuffling right on over to my room, dismounting, and trudging inside. After a hot bath, a fluffing of the curls, fresh jeans, and a little perfume, though, I felt absolutely great! Time for the rewards of the day—I hit the bar and saw the boys of the brotherhood grouped around the table, washing down popcorn with big, icy glasses of beer, looking like the last four guys who made it out of the Sahara after an air raid attack, grizzled, hairy, dangerous in thought and deed— but, to me, these guys were the Four Supremes. Supreme riders, adventurers, comrades in wind and sand—they looked good—and I felt privileged to ride with them.

The ride back to Albuquerque the next day was more of the same conditions—wind plus raingrooves—with rain and snow to spice things up. Rolling onto Interstate 25 North, I realized I had made it through my first big ride. I was now in familiar territory and was headed for the barn. A thrill of exhilaration raced through me. I put the hammer down and ran red hot until the needle vibrated at 90—and gave a rebel yell of triumph!

5

The sun lay like a friendly arm across her shoulder.
— Marjorie Kinnan Rawlings

*I want to know, Have you ever seen the rain
coming down on a sunny day?*
— Credence Clearwater

Rain, Sleet, or Snow...
I Ain't No Blinkin' Postman!

Weather is king when you take up the sport of motor-cycling. If you enjoy long rides, roaming around for hours on your bike, then the climate is going to play a leading role in the experience you have. It is inescapable. Most men and women who have been riding for awhile automatically pack rain gear and a few extra layers for added warmth in case they run into an unexpected change of conditions. Colorado is known for its unpredictable weather, as evidenced by the presence of the National Center for Atmospheric Research in Boulder. Meteorologists flock here to study our constant variety of weather patterns because they give them more frequent opportunities to record, to observe, to theorize, about scientific aspects of what we commonly call "weather." Want to know about the weather? Ask a biker.

Shortly after I began riding, my son commented that I had become a weather nut—more concerned about it than anyone he knew. He was right. Once you get caught riding unprepared during a major storm, your interest in weather forecasting soars. I try to keep riding all year, right through the winter, partly for the challenge of it and partly so I don't have to go through the hassle of winterizing my bike. I listen to the weather forecasts morning and evening, find myself checking for squall lines among clouds overhead or on the horizon, keeping an eye out as cloud types signifying a change sweep across our Colorado skies. On-the-bike training during my first road trip in New Mexico taught me it was also wise to note the direction and strength of the winds for the day. That habit has continued into my riding days in Colorado as, in both states, wind and rain can be an enormous challenge to contend with out on the road.

Early on, it became obvious to me that if I was going to ride around on a motorcycle and do any touring at all, I was going to get rained on, hailed on, and probably blown about now and then. It can be challenging and downright scary at times. You must learn not to panic, to stay steady, and to keep focused on the moment at hand. A good example would be a ride I took mid-summer. The weather had been on a record-breaking streak, day after day in the nineties and approaching 100 degrees, with only isolated sprinkles late each afternoon. We were in desperate need of a long, slow rain to bring down the high fire danger and to replenish supplies in some mountain areas. Pinecrest, a small community in the foothills of the Rockies, was out of water and residents had to truck it in. Raging forest fires had gobbled up thousands of acres of trees, foliage, and underbrush—and left animals and humans alike homeless. Forestry services were on 24 hour alert and all types of campfires were banned. Talk of drought was continual and more people than usual had an eye to the sky, hoping for rain.

With such a high probability of continued dry, hot weather, a couple of fellow motorcycling enthusiasts, Pam and Lee McLeod, and I, decided it would be a good time to start out early and ride through Rocky Mountain National Park and over Trail Ridge. Trail Ridge is a spectacular ride winding through inviting meadows and forests, dramatic geology and a variety of ecosystems, finally rising above the tree line to peak at more than 12,000 feet at a viewing station, gift shop, and restaurant perched on the Continental Divide. The 360 degree views are magnificent and it is a rare day when you do not see an abundance of wildlife, including deer, bighorn sheep, and grazing herds of elk. This day promised to be no exception. The forecast had been for hot and clear early, with ninety-plus temperatures and possibly the usual scattered afternoon thunderstorms. Instead, the morning dawned with a slight cloudiness over the mountains, but we set off optimistically, believing it would burn off and we would ride in the sunshine all day long. Taking the Fall River entrance into the Park, we saw fields of wildflowers, a few elk, a cautious doe stepping daintily out into the open, and an increasing number of tourists whose pace on the curving road indicated their unfamiliarity with mountain driving. It was glorious to be out and I was feeling good. Sinbad was running smooth and the day stretched out in front of us like an invitation. Having stopped at the summit for a cup of coffee and to soak up the full-circle views, we headed down the western slope for a quick cruise through Grand Lake, and then to lunch in Granby.

One of the great pleasures of riding is the feeling that you are a part of the world and not just an observer encased in the artificially heated or cooled environment of an automobile. The wind and sunshine are on your face and body, they act upon you and your machine, and you react, cutting through the day with a sense of exhilaration and freedom that cannot be found in a four-wheeled vehicle. The vibration, the power of the engine between your legs pulling you forward, the response of your machine to your weight shift or push and press of the handlebars, the roar and backfire of your pipes as you down shift or max your rpms throttling through gears—there is a joy in these simple mechanical actions that only a rider can know. It is a part of what is meant when someone asks a motorcyclist why they ride and the response is, "If you have to ask, you couldn't possibly know." It is a feeling of flying, yet with a difference. I have flown a variety of aircraft and enjoyed them all, but it did not have that same feeling about it except occasionally at take-off when you have full throttle, are barreling down the runway, then pull back slightly on the yoke and feel the plane glide up into the air with a sense of infinite possibility. That is as close as I have come to another sport feeling like riding a motorcycle down an open highway on a beautiful summer day.

That's how this day's ride with Pam and Lee started out; looking good, feeling good. From Granby, after fueling our bodies with cheeseburgers and fries and our machines with gas, we continued over Highway 40 toward Winterpark, planning to turn east at I-70 and homeward to wind up a 230 mile day. As we started off, we could see menacing black clouds building to the south of us and we reassured each other that we would skirt that trouble, like a kid saying "not me" when asked who ate the last piece of pie.

Just after Winterpark, a few sprinkles began to fall, but we optimistically rolled on. Soon it was coming down steadily and I was beginning to feel cold in my leather jacket over a tank top. After some miles of hoping the squall was going to pass through quickly, Lee signaled to pull over into a large, paved parking lot. We jumped off our bikes and dug into our saddlebags for our rubberized rain gear. Standing in a pouring, cold rain, with a helmet on your head, in full biker regalia—boots, chaps, bulky leather jacket and gloves—and contortioning your body into a rubber suit is also part of what biking is all about. But not the joyous part. I struggled to keep Velcro tabs from attaching to the wrong places, fought to get the legs of my suit over my boots without falling into the mud, stretched an elastic waistband over the entire bulk of myself, changed to warmer gloves, tucking them into the elastic wristbands for more waterproofing. Then, I got to do part of it all over again, as I realized I had forgotten to change from my sunglasses to my clear glasses for better visibility in the rapidly darkening day. By this time, I am the Pillsbury Dough Girl on a motorcycle—looking good, biker babe.

After consultation about whether to try to sit it out or continue on, we set off again. The clouds had not lifted, nor the rain lightened. The roads were slick, the traffic constant, with a lot more switchbacks to ride before the Interstate. We held our speed down and peered closely at suspicious spots in the road, anything that might shed traction. Even though I don't like riding in the rain, it seemed like it was going to remain manageable. Then the hail began, luckily only pea sized, hammering my helmet, dancing on the slick, shiny road, bouncing off my arms, wind and face shields. The rainfall increased and began to come down in sheets—I was spending part of my time wiping ineffectively at my face shield with my wet left glove, trying to keep my speed steady, watching traffic behind me and coming toward me around the curves. One way I deal with bad conditions when I am riding is by knowing how far ahead the next town is where I might find shelter, and checking the odometer frequently to see how close I am. I say over and over to myself, "Just 'x' number of miles to go. You can do it, Rosita; you can do it. Slow and steady. Just keep going; you'll get there." At times like this, the other drivers on the road are always more confidant than I am and crowd me from behind, urging me to go faster; this adds tremendously to my comfort level.

So, there I was, riding the dark side of cycling, summoning my courage to just keep on going, when I see a sign ahead and, the motorcyclists' sign of the devil, a line of orange cones—"Pavement Ends, 500 Feet." Oh boy, oh boy, I think, as I bump off onto the construction segment of the highway, weaving through cones, hoping no one in any direction is going too fast or had too much to drink. "What next," I say to myself, "I ain't no blinkin' postman! Leave the rain, snow and sleet to someone else. I just want to be home!"

As the interstate comes into view, the clouds lift, the pavement steams dry, and the heat tucks around us like a sodden blanket. Not wanting to stop until we cover some miles, we roll on, now beginning to swelter in our rubberized garments as humidity rises in our helmets and shields. A few miles down the highway we pull off alongside a river and dismount, struggle out of wet rain suits and gloves, clean off our shields, change to our sunglasses, and glance around. Hey, it's a beautiful sunny day, a great day for a ride—let's rock and roll. Ah, it's great to be on a motorcycle!

6

Adventure is worthwhile in itself.
— Amelia Earhart

I heard the Denver and Rio Grande locomotive howling off to the mountains. I wanted to pursue my star further.
— Jack Keroac

Solo

In Australia, the aborigines have a belief that everyone's existence is a "songline," which runs directly back to the source of all life from wherever they wander. I love the images this concept evokes. It makes me think about each of us writing a rainbow-tinted, unique melody with our lives, a jazz fusion of trills and riffs, patterns of notes dancing in combinations all our own. However, there is also a sense of destiny about their belief, as though we must follow the path we find ourselves assigned to. Have you ever dreamed you were in a room without windows or doors? A road without an exit? Many times the responsibilities of our work, our friends, and our families can leave us feeling like there is no central self that belongs to us alone. We must keep alert to the hidden crooks in the road, the secret windows we can climb through to explore alternative universes; in other words, the possibilities that present themselves to truly conduct our own symphony.

It seems to me that we often live our lives as though we are confined to a train track, with an assigned destination we go to and from each day. We take the same route to work, one we have determined is the "quickest." We go to the same supermarket, cleaners, gas station, and eat at the few restaurants we have determined are the "best." We see many of the same faces daily as we interact or pass by people on adjacent tracks to ours, all rushing along on essentially the same routes. But if one day we "jump the track," we might be surprised to find that it is not the disaster we have been warned about. There are countless other parallel or crisscrossing paths very different from ours, equally "best," perhaps more compelling than the one we originally selected. Perhaps our parents put us on the train at an early age; perhaps relationships have kept us there. When you jump the track you are confronted with people and ideas that play no role in your previous life. It is exciting and stimulating—and it changes our lives forever. That is what happened to me when I began riding motorcycles.

After I had been riding awhile, I found I was drawn to longer and longer rides—I just wanted to see what it would be like to see this area or that astride a motorcycle. Completely different from automobile travel, you are sensually aware of every dimension surrounding you—the rhythmic thrum of a bridge beneath your tires, the smell and feel of a moist hot wind after a rain, the immensity of stone towering over you as you wind through a canyon. It is a firsthand experience. You are not looking through glass and *thinking* about what it is like out there, applying previous knowledge or experiences to the visual, you are completely and fully present in the moment. And although you may be riding with others, your experience is uniquely your own within the group. As Robert Hughes, art critic for *Time* magazine once said in an essay, "The motorcycle is a charm against the Group Man [or woman, as the case might be]." In these days where we are increasingly identified not by our faces or voices, but by our "numbers" (social security, driver's license, account numbers, etc.), I find it important to my sense of individuality *not* to be confined to a category—neither by number, age, economic status, nor gender.

But riding a motorcycle with a group of other riders still contains pressures of conformity that I need to escape at times. As have most of us, I have spent my life feeling the subtle, sometimes not so subtle, weight of how others would like me to be, what they would like me to do. A part of that I have done willingly for those I love and I have enjoyed the warmth and comfort of fitting in and receiving societal and familial approval. But a part of me has always rebelled against molds based on cultural expectations. I want to reason things out for myself, make my own choices—and I am fully prepared to live with the consequences. Some of those issues arose in riding with groups when I became a biker.

I have some close friends I ride with—Pam and Lee McLeod, Dave Donnelly and Jay Wallace, to name a few, who just ride their ride and let me ride mine. There is no pressure, no need to perform to a certain standard—there is just the road, the enjoyment of the journey, the acceptance of each other as individuals who love the sport. I have spent some great days with these friends and hope to spend many more in their company. Outside of that, I much prefer to ride alone, to putt along at my own speed, testing myself when I choose, going where the road beckons, stopping where my curiosity carries me.

One of those solo journeys began as a long weekend late in August. I love those hot, dry summer days in Colorado when there is not a cloud in sight and I can pack up the bike and be on the road by 6:00 a.m. That morning, I headed south to Morrison in the foothills outside Denver where I often have breakfast at the start of a trip. I was having a little difficulty with my clutch lever, just getting used to a new friction zone, but it was no big deal and the day held so much promise for adventure. After eggs, bacon, hash browns and numerous refills of steaming coffee, with the sun on my shoulders and the sweet feel of freedom on my mind, I continued south down Highway 285. This is a beautiful road, winding through small mountain towns, curves sweeping into open, luscious views of valleys and sky, and the high desert beyond. Arriving in Fairplay I stopped for gas and checked my odometer, noticing I had just passed the 8,000 mile mark in my riding—it seemed amazing to me that I had ridden that many miles all in my first year. I drank a French Vanilla cappuccino and wolfed down a Twinkie, my sugar rush for the next leg.

Not many bikers were on the road. I considered stopping for the night at Valley View Hotsprings, a clothing-optional resort about seven, bone-jarring miles of gravel road outside Villa Grove, but decided against it since I was alone. As the afternoon wore on, I climbed into the mountains to the west toward South Fork; clouds began to roll in and it appeared inevitable that I would have to dig into that saddle-bag for the rain gear any minute. I had never been to South Fork before, just heard it was a popular fishing area; it is some of the most beautiful country I have seen—a multitude of rivers and streams, beautifully crafted log homes, and lush foliage. The 14,000 foot peaks to the west gave it a magnificent perspective, even as it began to rain.

Creede, Colorado. Just as appealing as I had always imagined—a small historic mining town situated at the mouth of a magnificent red rock canyon. Strength and energy seemed to emanate from the wet, sheer walls and they shimmered in the crisp afternoon light as I parked the bike and looked around. Wonderfully restored buildings, some upscale galleries, and a collection of the usual tourist shops lined the short main street.

I checked into The Old Firehouse Bed and Breakfast (actually a renovated firehouse). My room was furnished with antiques, the floors were dark, stained original planks, the bed dressed out in blue and white linens including a fluffy comforter and stacks of pillows. Everything was spotless, and the bathroom stocked with piles of terry towels. Downstairs is an old-fashioned ice cream parlor where you register and where breakfast is served each morning. The proprietor, when I was there, was a woman from El Paso whose family has long time ties to Creede, Katherine Brennand. She oversaw all of the renovation process herself, including doing much of the manual labor. I had dinner across the street, walked around looking in the shops and galleries, and visited casually with locals..

I find when I am traveling alone, I interact with people along the way much more than when I am with a group. You hear some amazing stories about how people come to live in a small, isolated community like Creede. I had planned my trip purposely to be there for the full moon, but the sky remained overcast until about three in the morning, when it shone brightly into my room, waking me. I got up and looked out at it's luminous face floating amidst the shredded clouds and thought about how much I was enjoying myself and my biking adventures, how unexpected it all was.

Friday morning. The day dawned sunny and I went down to clean the mud and road grit off Sinbad, took a couple of photos of him with that imposing, cinnamon-toned canyon in the background, had breakfast, chatted with Katherine, packed up and headed out.

Back in South Fork, I filled the tank and rode south to Wolf Creek Pass on Highway 160. Wolf Creek Pass, at 10,850 feet, is stunning! Wide sweeping turns and great road conditions—the views were so incredible that I finally pulled over to fully enjoy them—they were too special just to glimpse as I passed. Looking over country like that where you know so many historic events took place, where native Americans lived and thrived for centuries, where pioneers passed through in their daily push toward California, where cowboys still herd cattle, tourists ski, and thousands share the natural beauty of the region with an abundance of wildlife is like taking a long, cool, refreshing breath of pure oxygen. There is a sense of clarifying your lungs, your mind, and your heart.

From there through Pagosa Springs and into Durango, the weather was hot and summery and I was loving it. It was one of those days like melting chocolate savored on the tongue, when you know it won't be long before the passes will be snow-laden, that the perfect riding days are numbered before winter sets in.

And speaking of summer, that was the *end* of it for that trip! After lunch in Durango, I saw what looked like rain clouds higher up in the mountains toward Silverton where I was headed, so I pulled out my rain gear and suited up. It began to rain shortly after I set out, turned colder, then all hell broke loose as the skies opened and the road narrowed, twisted and turned. Huge rock walls rose to my left and, to my right, the sheer precipice left little room for emergency maneuvering. I slowed down, telling myself that I had dealt with rain before and could deal with this.

By the time it became apparent this was no passing squall, I was at Molas Divide (10,910 feet), more than half way to Silverton, and the thought of trying to make a U-turn in the middle of that tight road on rain-slicked black-top with low visibility for approaching cars seemed much worse than just going on. What had been a heavy steady rainfall became a forceful downpour, turned to pea-sized hail pummeling me from every direction. Thunder boomed and echoed off canyon walls, with lightning cracking immediately after.

Adjacent to a huge outcropping slightly overhanging the road, a rumble reverberated above and I was sure it would all come tumbling down to crush me. It wasn't a rockslide, thank God, but thunder so close it shook me in my boots, followed instantly by a crashing lightning strike in the canyon to my right that raised the hair on my neck! It was all I could do not to drop the bike and just curl into a ball in the middle of the road. I tried to stay slow and steady, talking myself through, looking for a place to take shelter. When I rounded a curve thirty minutes (and a lifetime) later, and saw Silverton below me, I felt saved; I was soaked through, miserable, and considerably shaken. There was no way I was going any further.

I checked into the Teller House. Although they eyed me with suspicion as I traipsed to the front desk in dripping boots, leather, and gear they were kind and my room a haven, looking out over the main street, warm and dry. A hot bath was just the ticket back to feeling pretty good about my survival and ready to explore. Silverton is the home of the Silverton Narrow Gauge railway—I heard later that the track had washed out in the storm and the daily train had to return in reverse all the way back down the mountain to Durango.

It continued to rain and by the time I headed over to the Handlebar Café and Saloon for dinner, my hair was sticking out in a frizzy jumble a foot around my head. One of the positive things about riding for me has been letting go of unrealistic concerns about my appearance when on the road. I have gotten comfortable with my often messy, dusty, sweaty self—my flattened or frizzed out hair, makeup long gone. I let people see me just as I am and I have set aside a lifetime habit of self-consciousness.

After such an adventurous and challenging afternoon, I can only tell you that the babyback ribs were that much sweeter, the pale ale colder, slightly biting, and it all went down easy. The next day would bring Red Mountain Pass (11,008 feet) and the so-called Million Dollar scenic highway—and the word from the locals was that they were blasting with dynamite up there even on weekends and drivers were experiencing up to one and a half hour delays, that the road was only one lane wide for part of the way and there were tunnels. Not a recipe to encourage a good night's sleep, especially if the rain continued. Hmmmm. Wasn't sure what to do—riding back the way I came didn't really appeal to me either. I hit the bed early and tried to read, but I was so exhausted the book kept falling out of my hands until finally I surrendered. I awoke several times during the night and heard the rain continuing to beat down on the roof and against the window panes.

Saturday morning. It was foggy and still raining lightly. I tried to call the Sheriff's department to check on road and weather conditions but got a dispatcher in Durango who said, "It's fine here!" and who didn't know squat about anywhere else—which did not prevent him from giving an opinion. No one I spoke to seemed to have a clue. I guess if you are not crazy enough to get on a motorcycle in this weather it's not an issue. Finally, around 7:30 a.m. after only a half-eaten breakfast, a nervous stomach, and a load of determination, I packed up Sinbad again, put on full cold weather stuff and rain gear, and headed north on Highway 550 toward Ouray. I didn't have that much experience with mountain conditions during bad weather and, not sure about the safest course of action, chose the route I had not seen because it seemed more appealing than to repeat my trip of the day before.

It was a ride from hell. I am sure it must be incredibly beautiful along that two lane winding highway among those haunting mountain peaks and valleys—*when the sun is out!* But it was raining steadily, it was cold, and there wasn't even a glimpse of Mr. Sun. I was lucky with the construction and blasting though—I had no wait at the first location and only a short wait at the second. The road was uneven and frequently patched, mud-slicked in places from mountain runoff, one lane each way except in the construction zones where it narrowed to one lane at a time. It twisted around and around, frequently back on itself in hairpin turns, with speed postings at times of only 10 mph. No need to caution *me*, for sure, as I was definitely putting along at minimum speed. To add to the fun, I had developed a problem with my idle—it would not go below 2,000 rpms when using engine braking and I had to start using my front and rear brakes more than I would have liked to keep at safe speeds. My mind jumped from one possible bad outcome to the next and I am certain my shoulders were up around my ears with stress.

Thankfully, traffic was light (how many other fools could there be?) and when it did stack up behind me I was able to let them get by rather than increasing my speed to an uncomfortable level. One lonely, beat up green pickup truck held way back behind me the whole way, probably had a driver just as scared as I was. After what seemed like an eternity, I rolled down into Ouray and parked the bike with the engine racing until I hit the kill switch. What a goofy deal that turned out to be—somehow I had accidentally pushed the choke on during my ride down the mountain and simply pushing it off solved the problem. Now *there's* a blonde biker moment!

By that time, I was sick to death of mountain riding and did not want to complete the circle back to Longmont through Glenwood Springs via Hotchkiss and Paonia. I opted for the longer but easier route through Grand Junction, where I knew I could get on I-70 and roll straight on home with plenty of lanes and good roads. It wasn't quite that easy, but I wanted desperately to be in my own bed that night, so I stopped only for gas and brief food breaks. The landscapes around Grand Junction and Palisades are dominated by a huge mesa in shades of cream and rose, with softly weathered folds of sandstone quilting its sides. It was a special, subtle, kind of beauty greatly contrasting with the sharp, dark and looming magnificence of the mountains I had just passed through.

Jammed with tourist traffic and semi-trucks heading for vacation or home ground, Interstate 70 was wild. From drivers speeding far above the 75 mile per hour limit, more than willing to mow you down if you impeded them in any way, to a shitload of sixteen wheelers flashing lights on the upgrades to signal they are barely moving, then barreling down the other side with brakes smoking. All this and more rain. Add two or three long tunnels with cars and trucks darting from lane to lane and tailgating me, one huge traffic jam just before my exit at Red Rocks (which turned out to be a semi that had steamed by me earlier, lost its brakes and taken out another vehicle), and the trip home was long, long, long.

I was dead tired and cold—the last thirty miles a challenge as I struggled to remain somewhat alert and cautious. When I rolled into my own garage in early evening, I was so dog tired I had to sit there a moment before I could haul myself off the bike and stagger into my welcoming home.

Why in the world, you might be asking yourself, would *anyone* want to subject themselves to this kind of danger, dirt and fatigue? The answer is, I don't know—what I *do* know is that it is the combination of experiences that keep you riding—the exhilaration of perfect conditions, the deep satisfaction of knowing you have pitted your self physically and mentally against challenging circumstances and survived.

I make my living sitting in a comfortable office thinking up words. I love my work, but it is the days spent tiring myself physically, being outdoors completely focused on my surroundings and the bit of highway in front of me that give me the deepest sleep, the best dreams, a feeling of well-earned rest. I come away from a road trip feeling a deeper understanding of my strengths and weaknesses, with a clearer perspective of my life and what truly matters.

Riding a motorcycle is not for everyone, nor is it a vehicle to self-awareness for everyone who does ride. The deeper experience comes from choosing any goal or activity that really interests you, in which you can immerse yourself completely and gain a measure of competence while still pressing the envelope. It is there, in the "zone," that you encounter your authentic self, and know somehow who you really are and what is essential to your life.

Biker Bars, Convenient Stores-
and Other Joints I've Known

Food. Road food. Ice-cold, raspberry-flavored tea in a sweaty bottle, inch-thick round wedges of real ice cream crushed between two huge chocolate chip cookies, and, of course, *chips*—flat, ridged, crispy, flavored ranch-style or spicy salsa. Or for the purists—"original" flavor with the taste of potatoes and grease that melts in your mouth and coats your fingers with coarse salt, causes you to poke one finger into the corners of the bag for just a crumb more! Remember Twinkies? That sponge-cake, cream-filled delight of younger days? Remember how the first bite into that delicious, sweet, preservative laden center made you want to wolf the whole thing down in one bite and reach for the next one?

There is something about being on the road with the sun and the wind in your face or on your shoulders, or fighting your way through adverse weather, that heightens the enjoyment of food and somehow gives "permission" to indulge in goodies you would never eat otherwise. Food most of us have given up. Comfort food. Although there is only occasional strenuous physical exertion when riding a motorcycle, perhaps because your whole mind and body are concentrated on operating your machine safely and competently, there is a sense of having "earned" extra calories, of needing them to keep your strength up for the road ahead. I can't recall ever seeing anyone I was riding with eat a salad or sip a simple cup of soup with half a cucumber sandwich. Seldom, if ever, have I heard a biker say, "Does that chili have animal products in it?" Or, "I'll take the tofu burger, hold the mayo!" The places where we eat on the road seldom offer sushi or mixed greens—unless collard greens cooked in bacon grease count.

Whether traveling across country or on a short day run, bikers look for casual places, the types of bars and diners where a trucker might stop for chow, where you can park in front and keep an eye on your bike out the window. Often we eat at places where it is known that bikers are welcome, even encouraged to hang out. A lot of eating between meals is done at convenience stores when you gas up your machine. You pull up to the pump, run up your $3-5 bill, roll on over to the parking area and go inside. We visit the restrooms, stroll the aisles, and choose our poison: sodas full of fizz, sugar and chemicals—the first big gulp bites its way down the throat in an explosively refreshing way; chips, ice cream, the aforementioned Twinkies, gooey snowball-shaped cupcakes in hot pink and covered with coconut, candy bars and nuts. Everyone has their favorite, their special weakness. No one ever asks "Hey, Lefty, how many grams of fat do you think that double size Mounds bar has in it?" We slurp, chomp, guzzle—and go. Total elapsed time: 15-20 minutes. We are on the road again.

But temporary refueling of body and machine at convenience stores, is only a very small part of the road food story for bikers. Bikers are road gourmets, the funkier the diner, the more we like it. We have a nostalgic streak in us that often glorifies the Fifties-style, Highway 66 diner. We prefer a Mom and Pop, family-run, cafe to a chain—but will not turn up our noses at a fast food restaurant when the need to feed is upon us.

Out on the highways of America, we indulge in the food of our childhoods, the food Mom might have cooked, nourishment before the health industry and the media conglomerates drove us mad with anxiety about every morsel we put into our mouths. Mounds of whipped potatoes with a lake of gravy ladled into their center, perched right next to a thick slab of ketchup-covered meat loaf (not likely to be

99% fat free ground beef). You make little "canyons" in the potato mountain and the rich brown gravy runs free to corral the meatloaf and the canned green beans nestled beside them. Golden-topped homemade, buttermilk biscuits the size of a *creme brulee* for four, smothered in white gravy and chunky with bits of pork sausage. We are not talking *white sauce* here, we are talking white *gravy* made with the drippings left over from frying up a batch of sweet and spicy sausage patties or links. Brown a little flour with the drippings, slowly add whole milk and watch the grease, milk, and flour thicken into a breakfast fit for a pack of hard riding bikers.

And don't forget chicken-fried steak, crisp and greasy on the outside, moist on the inside, reminiscent of many a payday childhood dinner. White bread—Wonder Bread—you can pour any left over gravy on this and sop it up! Thick crockery bowls of chili and beans covered with chunks of cheddar cheese and diced white onions, hunks of cornbread on the side and *real* butter!

Let us not pass over the lowly burger. Bikers love a burger, fries and strong black coffee or an icy beer (American, if you please, not one of those Micro-guys or foreign brews)—probably a Millers, a Coors, or a Bud. Bottle, no glass. Although a few of us are coffee freaks and addicted to our lattes and mochas, our Starbucks and Peabodies, most of us think there is nothing better after a cold, rainy ride than to stomp our way into a restaurant and gulp down a midnight black cup of coffee that has a faintly burnt aroma to it and is so thick and strong that it looks like engine oil. The first gulp scalds all the way down, then begins to spread out in the stomach, beating back the shivers and shakes from incipient hypothermia. Our ungloved, raw, red hands wrap around the cup in warm pleasure. It is the simple things that you become so keenly aware of on the road—many pretensions of so-called "civilized" or "urban" life just fall away.

But back to burgers. The bigger the better; no turkey, chicken, or tofu, faux burgers, just good old red meat in a huge, well-done slab. On a white hamburger bun, ketchup or mayo slathered on the top half, the hot, just-off-the-griddle grease of the meat soaking into the bottom. Cheese, chili, or bacon—maybe pickles, lettuce, and tomato. *Don't hold back on the fries*—hot browned wedges crisped and salty on the outside and mushy on the inside, ketchup drizzled on top. Oh, and don't forget a thick slice of white or yellow onion on that burger!

One thing about bikers, those who love onions eat them, those that don't do not complain. Conditions on the road tend to bring things back to basics in many ways: dust, sweat, grease or oil, wearing the same clothes several times, eating onions or garlic—people don't concern themselves as much with these things. They are too concentrated on the camaraderie, the landscape, and the thunder of their machines, to focus on such social niceties. And it is a relief to leave those concerns behind for a while.

Around the country there are roadside taverns or bars that cater to the motorcycling crowd. These are casual places, their walls often lined with biking paraphernalia—rusty parts, bandannas, photos of bike clubs, rally posters—all mixed in with a Biker Babe shot or two torn from a recent issue of *Easy Rider* or the like, and neon or lighted signs touting the sexy benefits of various beers. Most of these bars have been around for a long time, have boot-scarred wooden floors and booths, and smell slightly of booze and smoke. There is often a pool table or two, and an aura of parties past that blasted the roof off the place.

Every biker knows a few of these places where they can rest their road-stiffened bods, stretch their legs, count on some hot, solid food, a cold beer or hot cup of coffee, and a sense of being with family, of being accepted simply because you know what it is to ride the beast over the mountain. A woman who "rides her own" can stop in here and not be hassled. Oh, the men might offer a beer or strike up a conversation about her bike, but in general there is an air of respect for anyone who has been there and done that.

Since I began riding, I have enjoyed many a respite in some small, out-of-the-way café, a friendly chat with regular folks who work hard and serve good plain meals for reasonable prices. Most people seem pretty amazed when they find out I ride my own motorcycle and am off on a solo adventure. The women I meet are encouraging, take a small amount of personal pride in my achievement, and often look longingly out the window at Sinbad and then at the beckoning highway winding toward the horizon.

I have seen a few people turn up their noses and tighten their lips when I walk in, judging me by my black leathers, my disheveled appearance, the fact that I am obviously a biker (and, therefore, probably a BAD woman, and a threat to orderly, responsible lives). I don't mind. Most of my life I have fought against the judgments that my middle-of-the-road looks, my glasses, my bookish way of speaking and generally conservative dress have brought my way.

There is something deep in the heart of every person that yearns to be thought exciting, sexy, adventurous—to be seen as an individual beyond the career and family roles we have chosen and must manage. I have always wanted people to look at me and intuit my Walter Mitty fantasy figures, my heart, my inner self—but this has never happened. I find it immensely entertaining now when I am out with Sinbad riding my dreams—finding myself judged in exact opposition to the middle-aged, middle-class, white woman that I am.

8

You just keep alert, so as to capture the sizzling silk of the winged dream.
— Fatima Mernissi

I took to the open road in search of places where change did not mean ruin and where time and men and deeds connected.
— William Least Heat Moon

Eatin' Dust and
Living the Dream

My second season of riding, I decided to ride to California on my motorcycle. I planned for months, pouring over maps of possible routes, gathering information on highway conditions, distances between gas stations, talking to people who had done it. My head would fill with the excitement of such an undertaking, a trip that seemed to me to be daring and risky, but which drew me inexorably. I tried to persuade various other riders to going along, but either they did not have the vacation time or wanted to go at a pace much more demanding than I felt I could handle. Some encouraged me to go solo, others advised against it, particularly for a woman. As the date of my departure drew near, I began to have nightmares about breakdowns, highjacks, weather, road conditions, and rape. Finally, a week before I was due to start out, I called up the airlines and booked a ticket to fly out, giving up my hopes for a cross-country journey. I was not ready.

Giving up my dream of riding Sinbad to California left me feeling like a quitter and an inadequate rider. Those feelings were probably accurate for that time, and my decision not to do it was probably a sensible one given my experience and confidence level. Over the course of the following year, the dream of heading west still shimmered in the back of my mind. I rode a lot more miles, participated successfully in the Experienced Rider Course, began arranging my work schedule so I could take plenty of time off. My run from the Colorado Rockies to the West Coast *happened* in 2001.

I still had fears about facing challenges I could not handle out on the road alone, but the voices of Isabella Bird, Patricia McCairen, Anna Linnea, Craig Childs, William Heat Moon, Patrick Sykes, Betty Stringfield, and many others who have done solo journeys of one kind or another prodded me onward.[1] Women on Wheels scheduled their annual International Ride-In for Redding, California, and my fantasies expanded to include attending the rally and then riding on to dip my tired old boots into the Pacific Ocean.

My imagination loves to play adventure movies—and sometimes those movies are great fun, and sometimes they are suspense and terror, depending on my confidence level at the time. I spoke to many riders who had taken numerous cross-country runs, both in groups and solo—not many women, but some—and called members from national clubs I belonged to who lived in states I would be traveling through, who had ridden the roads I would be riding. I got my gear together. I had Sinbad gone over with a fine-tooth comb. Everything was good to go and I set a date for a July departure. Still scared, but determined, I told myself I would ride west, then if I felt it was all a huge mistake I would turn around and head home. I could always hide out for a few weeks and *say* I went!

Day 1 – The Adventure Begins. On the road by 6:15 a.m. I didn't sleep much last night. Fifty miles out, I had a hairy experience, just before the Eisenhower tunnel on Interstate 70 heading west—I was in the fast lane and Sinbad *quit!* I couldn't get more than a few inches off the road and couldn't get the kickstand down because the shoulder was muddy and angled downward into a ditch. Traffic was whizzing past, including semis, and I was freaking out. I put it in neutral and tried once more to start it—it turned over and ran beautifully the rest of the day! I will never know what the problem was but it seemed at the time that Sinbad was having second thoughts about heading West. You get a little superstitious out there alone.

As the day wore on I was feeling pretty good, excited about the adventure of days before me, and at Grand Junction decided to continue on to Green River—100 miles of horrible winds! Just shows you how quickly things can change from feeling very cool to feeling very scared. That stretch of the highway is not pretty. To paraphrase Carol Shields in *The Stone Diaries*, it is country you "wouldn't ask to dance a second waltz." By the time I checked in at the River Terrace it was 4:00 p.m. and I was whipped.

Utah has some of the most dramatic red rock country imaginable in its southern end—but what it doesn't have is decent coffee or ice-cold *beer!* Essentially a Latter Day Saints state, liquor of any kind must be purchased at a state liquor store and ordinary restaurants just don't offer it. As a child, I remember my mother longing for a decent cup of coffee on our annual visits to relatives in Moab—I swear they still make it out of boiled acorns or something. Without a cold beer to end the day and a hot, rich coffee to start it, I was in a constant state of deprivation throughout my time in Utah. Even so, this first day out ended with good food and a refreshing swim in the pool.

As I reviewed the events of the day I recalled bikers I had encountered along the way, mostly friendly with only one snotty and distinctly *unfriendly* BMW rider who refused to speak or chat, a young biker from Quebec touring the unfamiliar landscapes of the southwest and loving it, and nonbikers like the couple who had locked their keys in their car at a rest stop in the middle of nowhere, and the hotel workers from Chihuahua, Mexico, who were interested in talking about my trip. At 377 miles, it was a good start to the journey. No profound thoughts, I just tried to enjoy each moment, not solve anything or *do* anything. The sky, the red mesas, the snow-capped mountains—they were enough.

Days 2 – 7. Utah, Nevada, and Grass Valley, California. Heading out from Green River, I felt a little dispirited for some reason. It was 75 degrees at 6:00 a.m. but overcast with rain predicted. I think I was affected by early morning news about my route north toward Salt Lake being closed due to an accident between a motorcycle and a sixteen wheeler. Does anything positive ever come out of watching the morning news? Once I get going, though, on any given morning, the first one hundred miles are the best of the day—this second morning out on Highway 6 headed northwest, the landscape was striking—open, high desert, with mystical mesas outlined against the morning sky. After a few miles, I took a deep, relaxing breath, settled down in the saddle, and enjoyed the freshness of a day that stretched around me in shades of pastel, promising fun ahead.

In Price, I stopped for a hot chocolate and to put on warmer clothing. While parking my bike outside the coffee shop, a woman came up to me (the first of many I would meet over the following weeks) and questioned me about my trip. She gazed off down the street and said, more to herself than me, "someday…" then, enigmatically, "I live to be free…." I was struck by her longing, thankful for my own ability to make choices.

A man in the coffee shop put my nerves on edge by saying how dangerous the road was between there and Spanish Fort—I came to suspect over the time I spent talking with people on the road that those who wouldn't even try it are the ones that preferred you, particularly as a woman, not do it either. The next stretch of highway did have a lot of construction going on, and it was raining, but it was no big challenge.

In Spanish Fort I encountered the first outright hostility toward bikers in general and *women bikers* specifically. There is little that sets my teeth on edge more than those who judge you merely by your gender, your skin color, age or appearance. My experience in this part of Utah was that it was a land of tight-lipped women and sly-eyed men. Few would speak directly to you, fewer were friendly—the women were often downright hostile and the men did not smile or nod either, but never failed to check you out from the corner of their eye or after their women had passed by.

Wherever I have traveled around the world I have tried always to smile, to be friendly and considerate of local preferences. I have seldom encountered either rudeness or hostility in response, until I hit central Utah. I am sure there are tolerant, friendly people who live there, too—I am just telling you what I encountered. But then there was the car that paced me on the interstate—I looked over and two teenage girls were giving me big grins and thumbs up!

The next morning I headed for Nevada, stopping for gas and breakfast in Delle—a gas station and handful of trailers thrown down like dice in the middle of the salt flats. Riding alongside the Great Salt Lake in the early morning freshness, with sea gulls circling, egrets and herons feeding, was an exhilarating feeling, and I took it all in with great gulps of sea-scented air. At my second gas stop, I met Ed and his son, Chad, from Chico, California, heading home on bikes after visiting family in Idaho. Fun, nice men, and we rode together all the way to Battle Mountain; they kept me running wide-open, a little too hot for me at 80 mph, but it was fun to have the company and play a little road tag.

By this time strong winds had become all in a day's ride, along with construction zones, orange barrels and flags, hot-dogging semis, huge wheels grinding by and jet streams rocking you out of the blue. Open skies, tacky little towns— "passin' through" country. By this time I had traveled about 935 miles and it amazed me, seemed unreal, like I was in a dreamscape. It was what I had wanted—a series of days riding American highways on Sinbad, traveling light, talking to people met by chance, seeing new country and viewing old territory from a fresh perspective.

It was a long, monotonous ride into Reno, Nevada, but once I began the haul over the High Sierra Mountains on Interstate 80, I longed for such boredom. Between horrible, potholed roads, confusing, tight construction, extremely aggressive city drivers who would press down on you like their lives depended upon them getting past you in the next half-second, I was sweating bullets. Two lanes headed in each direction, one that was smooth but too dangerous due to wild drivers, the other more like crushed rock with rain grooves running crosswise, no shoulder and zero emergency maneuvering room. Taking a break in Truckee, I nearly swooned when I finally had a great cup of coffee in their charming, historic district. Back on the highway from hell, I rolled down the western slope and headed into Grass Valley for a few days of luxurious relaxation, gourmet meals, and the welcome company of family. I was ready to be off the bike for awhile, to enjoy this inviting community, to read, and visit.

Days 8 – 11, The Central Valley, Shasta, and Women on Wheels. Well, it was great to see the family, but I was ready to move on, to get back on the road. I had a terrific journey up through the Central Valley, leaving Grass Valley behind shortly after 6 a.m. A gorgeous morning with just a slight chill in the air and a well-maintained four lane road much of the way, meandering through rolling hills and clusters of oak trees. Yuba spelled breakfast and waffles. A mean spirited fellow sitting next to me felt compelled to relate each detail of every nasty motorcycle accident he had ever heard of, even after I asked him to stop. Adios, bad-time Charlie.

I loved the ride up Highway 99 to Chico—Cesar Chavez and John Steinbeck landscapes—small, shady towns, lush green produce farms, fruit stands. Nice easy pace on the road. I decided to go into Redding to check out the layout, then ask someone to suggest a nice scenic area to spend a couple of days before the rally began. It was over a hundred degrees and I was melting; I wanted to get up into the mountains for some cool relief. A fellow at the gas station suggested a loop through the Shasta area, ending up at McCloud for the night, then the next day I could look around that area and come back down for the Ride In the following day.

It was a perfect plan—there were good roads with frequent turnouts so I kept a leisurely pace and enjoyed the scenery. The heat was really taking it out of me by afternoon, and especially since I keep on my protective gear no matter what. There were trees as far as the eye could see; it was very dry, with some areas where a bad wildfire had passed through in recent years now showing only new growth. After an essential stop for delicious raspberry cobbler topped with vanilla ice cream and *pints* of water, I wet down my tee shirt, put a wet bandana around my neck, and headed north again. When you first see Mount Shasta, it seems like an illusion, a mirage of a mountain, looming out of the flats as it does in all its snow-capped glory! It was thrilling to set eyes on it.

I spent the night in the wonderful old McCloud Guest House—beautifully decorated rooms, comfy with air conditioning, and big claw foot tubs. A wide porch runs all the way along two sides of the old house and it is surrounded with huge, gnarled oak trees and vast expanses of lawn. What a perfect respite from the heat and dirt of the day. Friendly management, interesting guests, great breakfasts!

The following day I checked out the town of Mt. Shasta—big doings for the Fourth of July holiday—a street fair, music, food, and foot races. Saw more homemade birdhouses than I ever need to see again. The mountain itself looms majestically over the town. We had big storm clouds move in mid-day and it was very humid, but only a few sprinkles. I spent the afternoon in the porch rocker, dozing, reading, and listening to the birds sing vocal lead, with the cicadas as a doo-wop backup. Heavenly.

Around 5:00 p.m., I rode Sinbad south to McCloud River Falls—it was golden with light filtering through the trees, kids leaping from huge boulders into a deep, cold spring. I returned just in time for guest cocktail hour. I found those short interactions around meals, drinks, or at the gas pump interesting and they were just sufficient to keep me from being lonely on the road. Most people I met were astounded that I was on the road alone and had already ridden all the way from Colorado with more to go.

Independence Day—a propitious holiday to build this journey around. And a great day to meet up with three hundred or so other women at an all-women's rally. It was 115 degrees when I rolled back into Redding, and both Sinbad and I were ready to vapor lock. What an encouraging and thrilling sight to see all those women pulling up on their bikes from all over the country, many with bedrolls and camping gear. Here were women of all ages, sizes, and colors. They walked easy; they were clearly comfortable in their skins. Many had *years* of experience, riding the biggest full-dress motorcycles under all types of challenging conditions.

I felt a little self-conscious—my own skills seemed so wimpy compared to the competence of many of these women. Still, it was wonderful to see them, to ride with them the following day, to hear their stories about their trips and how they came to the sport. Like Ennis, with her trip across America on a 250 cc scooter—these women are determined to lead an engaged life. They ride all models and sizes of machines, some radically customized and gorgeous, some hard-ridden road bikes. Some of the women were young and buff, riding light-weight, hot-powered sports bikes with ease; some were not fit at all, but skilled and graceful in the saddle. What an electric charge to see them, each and every one!

Days 12 – 14, The Pacific Ocean and Oregon. If you love to ride the twisties, then don't miss the queen of them all—Highway 299 to Eureka—130 miles of twist and shout! What a way to begin a morning. By the time I reached Eureka, the temperature had dropped by fifty degrees and the fog had rolled in. I had to stop twice to add more clothing as I got colder and colder—from the in-your-face central valley frying pan to the mellow and mysterious green coastal zone in only a few hours.

I could not believe I was actually *riding* the legendary Redwood Highway; I had to keep saying, "I am really here! I am really doing this!" The sun came out and the fog lifted slightly, the Pacific beach was on my left and rolling in—I was totally stoked. Such a great feeling to think I lived the dream, I was *there*. I pulled over and trudged in my biking boots across the sand, just to dip them into the foam, and had a stranger take a photo of me with the ocean in the background, just to prove I made it.

The entire Redwood Highway serpentines through trees, gigantic tree fern, and heavy foliage so dense in places that signs suggest headlights even by day. This is tiring riding as I was cautious and pulled off again and again to let faster travelers go by. I missed a lot of the scenery due to a need to stay focused. I wanted to reach Grant's Pass, Oregon, before I called it a day—under these conditions, 310 miles is a very long day.

When I finally arrived, I found a place to stay along the river, sipped a beer while watching the water flow by in the hot summer dusk. Boaters skimmed the surface, here and there was a die-hard fisherman getting in one more cast, the setting sun flickered a golden goodnight. People stopped to ask if Sinbad was mine. It amazed me to see how interested and excited people were when they learned about my journey. It was fun to share it with them.

It had been a tough day and I felt my age—but it had also been a satisfying, glorious one, knowing I had ridden my dream. How often does the dream come true? You have to eat a lot of dust to get there, but then—oh, that moment!

Running North then East. I had ridden a meandering 2,000 miles more or less to get here. It was a little sad to realize there would be no more "West," that it was time to head north, then east—homeward bound. I had developed a rhythm to my days, loved getting up morning after morning, packing up Sinbad, running true in the clearest light of the day, smelling the earth giving off the night's moisture as the day warmed, stopping for the first cup of hot aromatic brew and a hearty breakfast. Of course, it is true that every single day of our lives holds the unknown, the unexpected, but somehow when you are out on the road it seems more apparent; it seems to promise excitement, romance and adventure.

These possibilities exist equally at home, but our routine lulls us into expecting the predictable. Imagining adventure is expressed so well in James Cowan's translation of *A Mapmaker's Dream: The meditations of Fra Mauro, Cartographer to the Court of Venice*: "…a world emerges not from the sea as an island appears to do after a long voyage, but from a state of enchantment inspired by the mind taking leave of itself."

The remainder of my grand circle odyssey took me over the Sisters mountains, through little towns, farming communities, up into Santiam Pass where the sky was crystal and eye-piercingly blue. The smell of pine and flowers enveloped me as I rode; it was a wonderful route right into the heart of Oregon to Redmond, where I spent a couple of nights with my lifelong friends, Chuck and Carolyn Koon.

Two days later, I was headed for Mount Hood and the northern state line to ride east along the powerful and historic Columbia River. I wound through dense forests, past parks, waterfalls just to the side of the road, and farms. Here and there I glimpsed the enticing sparkle of the river. At the Cascade exit, I took the toll bridge over the Columbia to Washington State. Made of steel, bars, and mesh, it was eerie to ride on. The water was visible far below through the slats of the bridge, and each groove grabbed at my tires as the wind buffeted us mightily. I didn't dare think about falling. I rode the river for miles along the Washington side; there were better views of the river and I realized its power and immensity, saw the windsurfers riding their boards, skimming along under the force of those world-class winds.

Once that night passed, I became keenly aware I was now headed home, that my days on the road were ticking away and it would soon be time to take up my everyday life. The flavor of a trip changes with that knowledge. I saw many more miles of interesting and beautiful country, re-entered Oregon to roll down its eastern edge and on into Idaho, visited Ketchum and Sun Valley, and met interesting people along the way. What is it about black leather chaps on a woman that drives a cowboy wild? Don't know, don't care— I just enjoy it! Ran into some rain here and there but never had to get the rain gear out the entire trip, something of a miracle in biker travels.

I rode south back into the northern part of Utah, which is lovely, then picked up Interstate 80 and headed dead east with the serious intention of running hot for the last two days as I burned back into familiar territory. By then I was eager for my own home, my own bed, clean clothes; eager to see my children, tell them about my adventures; ready to pick up where I had left off in my other life.

All totaled, I traveled 3,800 miles, through eight states, before I returned home that summer. I learned it takes a certain amount of mental toughness to deal with being completely on your own, depending upon a two-wheeled vehicle and a small bag of tools, clothing, and supplies for survival under constantly changing circumstances. If you are lacking that toughness when you begin, you will develop it quickly. A long road trip gives you ample time to review your life with an unsentimental eye. No matter how well the journey goes, decisions that affect your physical and mental well-being are frequently called for—and the immediate consequences of those decisions will be yours alone.

In my experience, many of us women defer to men in group situations. It is sometimes easier than bucking cultural expectations—and it is also sometimes *convenient* to have someone else make the choices. If things do not work out, it is not our fault, we are not responsible—and there is still someone else to come up with another solution to the fine mess we find ourselves in. Being our own bottom line at least occasionally is very important for our personal development—I firmly believe we must learn to lead as well as follow. It is strengthening and builds confidence when we are forced to think seriously and make decisions that will affect our own physical safety or the success of a chosen venture. Stretching the boundaries of our capabilities is inspiring and allows us to experience the joy of being the captain of our own voyage through life.

---

[1] For further information on these inspiring adventurers, *see*:

Bird, Isabella L., *A Lady's Life in the Rocky Mountains*, New ed. (Norman: University of Oklahoma Press, 1960).

Childs, Craig, *The Secret Knowledge of Water: Discovering the essence of the American Desert* (Seattle: Sasquatch Books, 2000).

Heat Moon, William Least, *A Journey into America: Blue Highways* (Little, Brown & Co., 1982).

Linnea, Anna, *Deep Water Passage: A Spriritual Journey at Midlife* (Little, Brown & Co., 1995).

McCairen, Patricia C., *Canyon Solitude: A Woman's Solo River Journey Through Grand Canyon* (Aventura Books, 1998).

Stringfield, Bessie. One of the first African American women to challenge racial and gender barriers in motorcycling. She began riding in the late 1920s. For more information, *see* http://www.boarhog.com/stringfield.htm.

Symmes, Patrick, *Chasing Che: A Motorcycle Journey in Search of the Guevara Legend* (Vintage Books, 2000).

9

*I could not, at any age, be content to take my place by the fireside and
simply look on. Life was meant to be lived. Curiosity must be kept alive.
One must never, for whatever reason, turn [her] back on life.*
— Eleanor Roosevelt

*Life is about not knowing, having to change, taking the moment and
making the best of it without knowing what's going to happen next.*
— Gilda Radner

Time is a dressmaker specializing in alterations.
— Faith Baldwin

Seasons

I grew up in a small, rural town in southern California
in a time when citrus trees stretched out in shining rows
across hill after tawny hill, and open stretches of coastline
flowed unlittered and undeveloped down to the sea. In the
fifties, the sky overhead came unadulterated from an artist's
paint tube, slabbed on with a palette knife in great, brilliant
streaks of cerulean. I played under that sky during seem-
ingly endless days of sunshine burning down on the alfalfa
fields surrounding my house, never thinking that one day
that sky would be white and sulfurous with pollutants; that
those shining hills would be crammed with tracts of look-
alike houses, and that the coastline would cease to be unfet-

tered. It was also under that brilliant sky that I went for my first motorcycle ride, as a passenger, hugging tightly to the slender waist of a biker boyfriend, as we leaned and curved through green hills between Elsinore and Perris. It felt free and exciting, as though I were beginning the larger-than-life existence I knew awaited me.

Many years have gone by since those days, but I have rediscovered that childhood sky and the feelings those rides evoked during my travels through all the seasons in Colorado. The thrill of learning these new skills has reinforced the importance of fully engaging life at every stage. I have long felt that each decade of our lives has a special task, or purpose—and to leave it unfulfilled is to drag those issues onward into the next.

For example, in my own life, my twenties were about trying to get taken seriously in my career and by my family; they were about laying the educational groundwork for the first and learning to handle my emotions in regard to the second. I married very young and struggled with all the responsibilities of marriage and motherhood. My thirties were focused even more intensely on my career in some ways, but because I had not had much time or money to play in earlier years, they were also a time to chase some dreams, to experiment with who and what I hoped to be.

I think, for many of us, the decade of our forties is the time when we must resolve any issues we are still struggling with in our relationships with parents and family. We must decide for ourselves who we have become, use our *own* measuring tape to determine our worth. It is a time to sort out what our values *really* are, not what we give lip service to, and to start thinking about how to best express them within the framework of our personal and professional lives. After decades of hard work in all these areas, the fifties are wonderful years for self-realization. They are years for refining our more authentic self. These years can be thoroughly enjoyable and comfortable if you have done your homework over the previous decades. It is a time for discarding ideas and behaviors that you adopted earlier in life to suit other people, a time for knowing more about who you are and what you have to offer your family, your colleagues, your friends, and your community.

Personally, I have also had to come to terms, or at least try, with my mortality; I have realized that time is the most valuable asset I have—and how I spend it, the most critical decision I make on a daily basis. If you are putting off doing things that you have dreamed of all your life, I can only say "*Stop that!*" Reach out now for a measure of that achievement.

These days, I make a point of riding my motorcycle during every month of the year here in the Rocky Mountain state. Most years it is very doable. I have shared some stories with you about the winds of spring, the pleasures and challenges of summer and cross-country riding. Fall is the luminous, dazzling season here. Diane Ackerman, a writer I admire whose subject is natural history, says, "There is a way of beholding nature that is itself a form of prayer." That is how a fall day in the mountains makes me feel, that it is a sacred gift to behold such beauty.

One crisp afternoon, I rode up to Estes Park, a community poised at the edge of Rocky Mountain National Park, had lunch, and decided to return home through a little side route called Devil's Gulch, which switchbacks down into the little mountain town of Glen Haven, connecting back up with Highway 34 to run alongside Big Thompson River and on into Loveland. This is a wonderful scenic area and in the Fall few people travel this way on a week day afternoon, so I could take my time and just absorb the massive gray, lichen-covered slabs of rock and rushing river, the reds and yellows of the foliage.

Quite suddenly it seemed, clouds moved in, it became chilly, and the entire mood of the moment changed from exhilarating to sinister as black, dead leaves scurried like tarantulas across the road and the day darkened. Have you ever been somewhere familiar then looked around and it all looked strange to you, like you had crossed over into the Twilight Zone? Within minutes, that is how this ride went. Areas I had always found charming felt threatening, I was keenly aware no one was around, and it didn't feel like welcome solitude any longer, it felt like loneliness. I began to feel eager to get off the mountain; then, in the way of life with its constant change and unexpected joys, I rounded a corner, the sun moved out of the clouds and warmed me. A gusty breeze rustled through the Aspens on either side of the road and I was immersed in a cloud of fall leaves, swirling around me like gold dust—it was magical, something you could never experience in an enclosed vehicle.

This is why I ride, for these are epiphanous moments, glorious to recall, delightful and delicious to experience. Each season has them. Each year I ride, as I think back over the months, these memories appear like classic paintings in my mind, richly hued in subtle shades of browns, charcoals, reds, yellows and blues—some bolder and more outspoken than others, some in softer grays of fog and mystery. It is their luxurious subtlety, depth and variety that aligns itself with the tenor of my life and draws me back to explore them again and again.

Calling this final chapter "Seasons" to tell you about what it is to ride a motorcycle in this glorious state year round is half its message. Although it is hackneyed to use the metaphor of the seasons to symbolize the stages of our life, like all good sayings and timeworn metaphors, there is more than a kernel of truth in their use. Obviously, I am in what would statistically be called the "autumn" of my life, having squeezed every drop out of spring and summer. I feel like I am still in summer, but that is an illusion.

My least favorite season is winter. Oh, the first snowfalls are exciting and lovely, and cover a multitude of leftover yard chores and bleak landscape—but it is often too cold to spend much time outdoors. Then, there are a couple of months in Colorado after all the beautiful leaves of fall have gone the way of the rake and before those snows again do their magic—an "in-between" time that seems depressing to me with its barren trees and brown hills and yards, everything dry, the excitement of the brilliant golds and reds finished. I have to remind myself that the sap still runs sweet in winter's plain, spare limbs. I don't much like to think about winter then as a metaphor for the last period of my life. When it comes, I hope to face it with courage, élan, peace in my heart and mind. In the meantime, the autumn season in Colorado is considered by many to be its most hauntingly beautiful, tinged as it is with the foreknowledge of the winter that lies ahead. It is a season of golden light— and a season for riding one's dearest dreams on down the road.

Imagination is the highest kite one can fly.

— Lauren Bacall

Parting Comments

This book was not intended to be a travelogue, a geography lesson, or an instruction manual on how-to-ride a motorcycle. My intention has been to offer a story about how I rode my own dream—and hopefully to encourage others to reach for theirs. Sometimes a person's life ticks away like an oven timer, continuously on the move without ever leaving its circumscribed course. Stepping away from those borders and limits gives life intensity and richness and I highly recommend it.

The Roadmap to Your Dreams that follows these comments will set forth a few ideas about how to clarify which possibilities in life are *your* dreams and which are simply the expectations of society and those around you. When you can sort that out and start making choices that more accurately reflect your personal thoughts and beliefs, when you begin to stretch toward your own horizons, it will truly bring more joy into your life. I wish you luck and great times.

I want to comment on the quotations throughout the book. A lot of thought was put into their selection and each has special meaning for me. I hope you will find a few favorites for yourself. Several people advised me to use only quotes by women. I considered their advice and then decided that one of the things this book is about is *not* confining people to categories based upon age, gender, race, or anything else. I have been inspired by both men and women and take the ideas that guide me wherever I can find them. Of course, I sometimes feel that other women can capture my feelings and experiences in life more deeply than a man might, but I have known some supreme men.

Were you disappointed that I skimmed over the spicy parts: sex, drugs and rock and roll? I apologize for skipping those details, but for the protection of anyone who might recognize himself, I decided to leave that up to your imagination. I do want to say, though, that I have a strong interest in two of the three. There is no shortage of men on the motorcycling circuits and, as Pam Houston's book expresses it, "cowboys are my weakness."[1] And, yes, mama, desperados *do* dance! Which brings us to rock and roll.

My heart will always beat faster, my soul sing, when I hear the first few bars of "Great Balls of Fire," "Hound Dog," "Only You," "Blueberry Hill," "Hotel California," or "Long

Tall Sally," (to name just a few)— Jerry Lee Lewis, Elvis, The Platters, Fats, The Eagles, Little Richard—plus Willie, Waylon and the Boys, "Bird Dog" by the Everly Brothers, Fifth dimension's "Aquarius, "Ruby Tuesday" from the Stones and, more recently, just about everything Eric Clapton ever did. But while all that drives me wild, it is neither the great-looking men in tight jeans and chaps, nor the legendary traveling tunes of rock and roll that attracted me to motor-cycling. The biggest thrills have come from the sense of ex-hilaration and freedom when I am on the road, from my feeling of competence with something mechanical, from having brought my fantasy to life. Thank you for coming along for the ride.

1 A fun read: *Cowboys Are My Weakness*, Pam Houston (Washington Square press, 1992).

Don't let anyone rob you of your imagination, your creativity,
or your curiosity. . . . it's your life. Go on and do all you can with it, and
make it the life you want to live.

— Mae Jemison/Astronaut

A dreamer—you know—it's a mind that looks over the edges of things.

— Mary O'Hara

Roadmap to Your Dreams

<u>*Step One: Naming the Dream*</u>. Philosophers and an-
thropologists often speak of "naming" as a way of differen-
tiating one thing or concept from another, a way of giving
it spirit and life within a culture. It gives emphasis and
power to an idea, person, or thing to name it, to draw it
forward from the crowd of generics and brand it with a
special significance. For example, a cat is just a cat until she
becomes "Ruby," "Lucy" or "Stormy." Then she is personal,
your cat, the one who nestles beside you while you watch
TV, curling her paws contentedly beneath her and hum-
ming her song.

The same is true for our dreams. At first they are simply a piece of mental embroidery we work on in our spare

moments, a little flash here, a little drama there—but once we say out loud, "I want to ride a motorcycle, by myself, across country, day after day on the beckoning highway!"— it is then that we have given the idea enough power that we can begin to move toward its accomplishment, its reality. Take that important first step and identify your dream, write it down, imagine its accomplishment, tell someone you trust to be supportive. Give the dream power!

Step Two: One Size Does Not Fit All. Okay, you have a dream. One you have often fantasized about but felt might be a little bit out of your reach. You are going to become the lead guitarist for The Stones—*sure* you are! Not to shoot that idea down in flames, because who knows what might be possible once you have dared to let your special desire out of the box? But, for most of us, we must take some time to size our dream to fit our circumstances. On the other hand, don't be afraid to aim beyond what you presently think you can accomplish—stretch your neck out a bit. A dream is not an ordinary goal, it is a wish your heart makes.

No one could ever have convinced me just one year earlier that I would be able to ride a motorcycle on my own, that I would ride more than 11,000 miles on it during that first year, and ride half way across the United States solo just a couple of seasons after that. So, don't let anyone sell you on a dream that is just too small for your big fat wish!

Step Three: First Steps and Timetables. How do you know whether it is too big an aspiration? Write it down, like a goal or a New Year's resolution. Write down where you are now by comparison—and don't just write "nowheresville" on that paper—I mean write down what skills or talents you already possess in some measure that are a part of what will be needed to get you where you want to be. Take the big view and then the small view; see where your dream resides between the two.

Say you want to learn how to ski, you are sixty years old and have never tried it, you have just seen people do it on TV and think it would be exhilarating to fly down a beautiful mountain like that, and the clothes are so cute. Think about it: have you stayed pretty active? Do you do aerobics or dance, or some other activity that requires balance and agility? That's a great starting point. If you don't have any stamina and you want to get into a sport, you will need to get into an exercise program as a first step.

Find out everything you can about whatever it is you want. Talk to others who have gone before you and succeeded. If expense is a problem, start saving. You will probably need instruction from someone, so start searching for the right person to boost you toward your goal. In other words, write down everything that will be needed to make your journey. Then break all of that down into steps, from the very first one—which may be picking up the phone and calling ski resorts to see who has an instructor who specializes in teaching mature beginners. Read the most exciting books you can find about people doing what you want to do—and read the experts on how to do it. Visualize yourself doing it each step of the way.

Step Four: Going Against the Grain. A key component of every step toward your dream goal is not to allow yourself to be deterred by people around you who think (and say) you shouldn't do it, you can't do it, you are too old, too weak, too Brunette, whatever. You have done a lot of living by this stage of the game and you have probably already survived many difficult challenges. You have the experience to figure this out, to analyze your findings and determine what level of achievement you are going to strive toward. Push a little beyond what you think you can do—you can always change your mind.

Begin with the first step and see how you feel about it. Expect to feel discouraged at times—it is a part of the process. Dreams are a magical thing, often taking on a life of their own. Remember that the journey is as important, and sometimes more important, than the destination. Keep in mind that, even if each step you take is a baby step, if you continue to face in the same direction, you will eventually arrive at your destination. There is no timetable. As you progress, watch other doors open—dreams and wishes evolve and what you want to achieve may change. Allow for that but, always, always, choose for yourself.

Step Five: Dealing with Fear. I don't know about you, but for me every single new adventure contains about umpteen million things to worry about. It is in this area that my imagination is not my best friend because I project consequences of my actions that far exceed reality. When I first began riding Sinbad, I saw potential accidents everywhere and couldn't sleep the night before I was going to ride because of it. As I gained skill and confidence, I got those concerns down to a nice little backpack size containing a reality-based understanding of the risks of the sport, but also the knowledge that I have been trained to deal with most situations and cannot control the others.

Changing tracks, setting a new course into new territory gives us an opportunity to expand our knowledge of ourselves. A part of that is learning how to deal with our concerns that we might fail to reach our goal, fear of being injured or worse in the pursuit of a sport, fear of appearing silly, stupid or less than the perfect image we would like to project. And fear of how that will expose us to those who scoffed. The best antidote to fear is knowledge. Whatever you have determined to do, educate yourself about its pluses and minuses.

If your fears are really holding you back, make a list of them on one side a sheet of paper—then, across from each one, write down something concrete you can do that will help alleviate it. Be realistic but do not underestimate yourself. Keep in mind that all challenges offer a broader range of choices than it first appears. Consider your options.

Step Six: You Are Not alone. Whatever your dream, find a group of people to associate with who will support and encourage you, even help you along the way if they already have those skills. Consider forming your own group of a few people, each of whom will choose a goal, meeting once a month or so to discuss progress and brainstorm ways to break through roadblocks. Avoid all naysayers, most especially those who are telling you things for "your own good" or who try to shame you for being so selfish as to want something new in your life.

Friends and family often rely on us to continue to be the familiar person they have always known—change can frighten them, sometimes make them feel insecure and wonder what other hidden secret desires you have that may surface at any moment. Be firm, stand your ground, but be kind. You know yourself better than anyone—are you really a selfish bitch without a care in your heart for those around you? I would bet not—don't let other's pessimistic remarks spoil your day. Think rationally about what they are saying; evaluate for yourself whether the comments have merit. You are not a kid—rely on your judgment and intuition, developed over many years. You will know in your heart if this is the time to go from longing to living your heart's desire. Trust yourself.

Step Seven: The Journey's the Thing. Whatever you choose, don't be too focused on the end goal. Once you have made your personal roadmap, focus on the journey, on each step along the way. Appreciate the significance of each. Be fully present in each of those moments. When I am out hiking, for example, I may have a certain point that is my goal for the day. I have sometimes found myself walking briskly along, watching my feet, and thinking about something else, somewhere else. I have a silly thing I say to myself every now and then: "Look up, look down, look all around."

Of course, you can probably think of something more profound or more entertaining to say to yourself, but the point is that I want to see where I am at the moment; I don't want to miss that starchy white cloud overhead, that tiny, star-like flower growing just to the left of the trail, the smell of the earth after a summer storm has passed through. It takes time to develop this habit of being fully present, but the rewards are intense. Sometimes the goal ahead turns out to be a mirage, others a miracle—but I promise you that the journey is the thing.

Step Eight: Every Dream Has Its Season. Life is change. Surely by now you have seen that. It is our nature as humans, I think, to try to get everything into just the perfect place and insist it stay that way—it makes us feel more secure, less vulnerable to unexpected disaster. But that is totally an illusion. Helen Keller, who had many challenges in life, believed that, "Life is either a daring adventure or nothing at all. Security is mostly a superstition. It does not exist in nature."

Many a change has come my way over the decades. I have often taken refuge in denial and struggled terribly with accepting new conditions, losses of people I loved, betrayals, rejection, and my own physical or mental shortcomings. I have slowly made progress toward taking each day as it comes my way, living the moment. But, as someone once said to me, "Seize the day, but don't hold it by the throat!" Hold the things you love lightly so they can breath. Look at your dreams and see what measure of them you can bring to life—and which you need to let slip through your fingers. Be an explorer in your own life, continue to try new things and push the limits of your horizons.

I wish you blue skies, green lights and safe journeys.

Acknowledgments

No book is created in a vacuum, and *DREAM RIDER* is definitely not an exception. Many people contributed to the effort and, without each of them, you would not be holding this book in your hands. They each have my sincere gratitude.

I started keeping a log of the places I went and the miles I rode as soon as I began to ride a motorcycle. It was a habit formed as a pilot and as a scuba diver—both activities enhanced by keeping a record of my experiences. I love to read back over these "trip diaries"—they bring back so many wonderful memories that may have slipped my mind. Although I have wanted to write a book for many years, it was not until I began to understand the ways in which touring the country on a motorcycle mirrors a great many of life's challenges in general that I began to think about writing this book. My longtime friend and former writing teacher (herself an author of several books), Diane Gage, agreed to read the first few chapters and give me some input. Because

I know the quality of her own work and highly value her opinion, her enthusiasm and encouragement have carried me along toward publication, even through the low times when it seemed I would never reach my goal.

Two editors whose professional standards I particularly admire—Jody Berman and Dianne Lorang—looked over earlier versions and gave me thoughtful, candid suggestions that helped immensely. The Boulder Media Women, an informal group engaged in the media professions, also provided support and counsel on a number of issues—most especially Evelyn Kaye. Dan Kennedy of Whitehorse Press took the time (so exceptional in the fast-paced publishing world) to write a personal letter of encouragement and to offer some sage advice about market placement. I want to thank Standish Lawder for so generously allowing us to set up a photo shoot for the book jacket in his studio at the Denver Darkroom, my long-time riding buddy Dave Donnelly for helping with all the heavy lifting, and Peter Warren for his diligent and skillful creation of the digitalized cover photo. Laurie Prindle was supreme to work with on the cover's graphic design and implementation; she tutored me patiently on the interior layout, and I highly recommend her.

Special recognition goes to John Russell, owner of Rocky Mountain Motorsports in Loveland, Colorado—a gifted mechanic who has taught me to understand some of what makes these iron horses run. To all those I have ridden with across this beautiful state of Colorado and beyond, including the members of Front Range Gold and Women on Wheels, you have been great company. And, always to be remembered, are the many people whose names I don't know, but met in towns and on the highways across the country. They were kind to me, told me their stories, made me feel safe, and added to my deep appreciation of the American landscape.

On a personal note, my family and friends were enthusiastic and supportive throughout the process, especially my daughter, Katie, my son Steve and his wife, Linda. It is their love and constancy that guide me like the North Star on my own true journey.

The Dream Riders

Anibas, Alice
Bacome, Mary
Bell, Jane
Caffrey, Jan
Carstens, Rosemary
Cichy, Lillian
Cinelli, Mary Rose
Cole, Susan
Collins, April
Deshotel, Judy
Diemond, Gayle
Dunning, Nancy
Durm, Penny
Earley, Kathleen
Elliott, Judy
Gunter-Goodman, Linda
Hartman, Fran
Hartnett, Bette
Harvey, Nancy
Hauck, Bonnie Lee
Heselton, Mary Lou
Janik, Vickki
Jarecki, Georgene
Jennings, Joan
Jensen, Shirley
Josselyn, Priscilla
Joyner, Callie
Killian, Janice
Kirk, Michele

Lewis, Linda
Lindeen, Glenda
Marsh, Vicki
McCann, Carol
McCluskey, Sara Jean
Meyer, Karen
Miller, Carol
Miller, Marie
Montgomery, Donna
Patterson, Shari
Pesce, Sherrie
Pschirer, Marlene
Redfearn, Kay
Reitinger, Kathy
Sammis, Carolyn
Sarka, Sharon
Shields, Linda
Slater, Mary
Smith, Marcie
Sofia, Maria
Stanley, Bobbie
Statz, Linda
Swanson, Pam
Taylor, Susan
Tracey, Barbara
Via, Melba
Williams, Janat
Zerkle, Anne
Zimmerman, Gloria

About the Author

Rosemary Carstens is a freelance writer and editor, with a head full of daydreams and a penchant for travel and adventure. Continuing to take on new challenges in her fifties has led her to believe that others can also do more than they ever imagined, at any age. She lives in Longmont, Colorado with her latest ride, *The Road Goddess*. This is her first book.

Did you enjoy this book?

Would you like additional copies for friends and family?

Turn this page for an Easy Order Form.

EASY ORDER FORM

Black Lightning Press
914 Hover Ridge Cr.
Longmont, CO 80501
303.776.8400 - Voice
303.776.8633 - Fax
Book@TheDreamRider.com

Postal Orders: To order directly from the author, please complete this form and send to the above address with your check made payable to Rosemary Carstens in the amount of the book plus postage and handling. If you want it autographed, please include instructions on how you would like it signed.

If you prefer, an account has been set up for the author at **www.paypal.com**. Just click on "Send Money," designating the recipient as Book@TheDreamRider.com, and you will be able to use a credit card for book, postage and handling. Please include the following information in the comments section:

Please send _____ copies of *Dream Rider: Roadmap to an Adventurous Life* to:

Name: _____

Address:_____

City:_____ **State:**_____ **Zip:**_____

Telephone:_____

EMail Address:_____

Note: Book Price is $15.00. Shipping is $4.00 for the first book and $2.00 for each additional book. U.S. only. International rates available upon request. ISBN 0-9740546-9-0